INSPIRED COOKING DEUX

A Collection of Short Stories and Recipes by

Clay Morris

Clay Morris

INSPIRED COOKING DEUX by Clay Morris
Published by Empoword Publishing Worldwide
Copyright © 2022 by Clay Morris
Inspired Cooking Deux: A Collection of Short Stories and Recipes Shared by Clay Morris
by Clay Morris

Printed in the United States of America. All rights reserved solely by the author. The author guarantees all artwork, images, recipes, and contents are original and do not infringe upon the legal rights of any other person, entity, or work. The author further guarantees that any content that is not original is rightfully and truthfully cited to the best of the author's knowledge. No part of this book may be reproduced in any form without the permission of Empoword Publishing Worldwide and the author. The views expressed in this book are not necessarily those of the publisher.

Empoword Publishing Worldwide
17127 Wax Rd Bldg A
Greenwell Springs, LA 70739
www.EmpowordPublishing.com
(225) 412-3130

One-touch Editing

This book has been edited by **One Touch Editing Services** (O.T.E.S.) located in Baton Rouge, LA (225) 304-1864. www.*OneTouchEditing*.com

This book is protected by the copyright laws of the United States of America. The scanning, uploading, and distribution of this book or any part thereof via the Internet or any other means without the permission of the publisher or author is illegal and punishable by law. Please purchase only authorized editions and do not participate in or encourage the electronic piracy of copyrighted materials.

The purpose of this book is to motivate and inspire the reader. The author and publisher shall have neither liability or responsibility for anyone(s) with respect to any loss or damage caused, directly or indirectly, by the information contained in this book. Unless otherwise noted, all scriptures referenced in this book are in The Holy Bible New King James Version Copyright © 1982 Thomas Nelson, Inc., Publishers. Used by permission.

ISBN: 979-8-360-71981-6

TABLE OF CONTENTS

Dedication 1
Introduction 2
    Alabama White Sauce 3
    Poor Boy's Burnt Ends 5
    Poor Boy's Burnt Ends Grilled Cheese 8
    Smoked B & B Burgers (Bacon & Blue Cheese) 11
    Stuffed Smoked Meatloaf 14
    Smoked Split Chicken with Alabama White Sauce 17
Be a Good Neighbor; It's Contagious 19
Making a Difference and Impacting our Impact Zone 22
After the Storms 27
What's Next? 32
10/10/80 36
    Breakfast Bowls 40
    Vacay Biscuits & Gravy 43
    Crawfish Cheese Omelet 45
    Oven-Baked Cheesy-Meaty Breakfast 47
    Mama G's Crawfish Pie 49
    Granny Ruth's Crawfish Etouffee 52
Mom – What a Woman! 54
Sunshine 60
This Isn't an All-You-Can-Eat-Place! 64
    First Born 68

Hang in There, Son!	73
Bonus Kids	77
A Champion's Heart	81
Crispy Parma Pork & Pasta	86
Garlic-Parmesan Chicken Wings	90
Parmesan Shrimp Avocado Garlic Bread	93
Roasted Pork with Garlic Parmesan Cream Sauce	96
Sunshine Shrimp Pasta	100
Bacon Wrapped Buffalo Chicken	103
Baked Stuffed Chicken Breast	105
Italian Chicken Pasta	107
Christmas Traditions	109
High School Days – The Good Ole Days	113
It's More than a Workplace	118
Suicide – The Aftermath	123
You Can Do It! Don't Quit!	129
An Investment with Great Returns	135
Turkey Taco Lettuce Wraps	141
Street Corn Dip	144
Meat & Cheese Rollups	146
Buttermilk Blue Cheese Dressing	148
Buttermilk Ranch Dressing	150
Shepherd's Pie	152
Spaghetti for 50	155
Red Beans & Rice – The Monday Special	158

DEDICATION

This book is dedicated to my loving, supportive wife. Without her by my side, I would not be the man I am today. Thank you, Michelle. You are amazing!

Introduction

Inspired Cooking Deux is a continuation of my first project, *Inspired Cooking*. We have so many stories and experiences in our life that we can share, and this book was inspired more because of the stories than the recipes. Although I know you will find the recipes in this version to be just as tasty as the ones previously published, I pray that the combination of recipes and stories moves you to a place of inspiration and encouragement to pursue whatever vision or dream you have.

One thing I have learned through the book writing process is this. Everyone has a story, and everyone has someone that needs to hear that story. Friends, I encourage you to put your story out there. Use your story to impact others. Use your story to add value. Use your story to make a difference in someone's life.

My story just happens to include recipes and cooking. I know you will enjoy the stories from my life and the many recipes I've shared. Get ready to be inspired and be blessed as you turn the pages of *Inspired Cooking Deux*!

Alabama White Sauce

Ingredients

- 2-1/2 cups mayonnaise
- 1-1/4 cup apple cider vinegar
- 2 tsp. Kosher salt
- 2 tsp. sugar
- 2 tsp. garlic and pepper seasoning
- 1 tsp. garlic powder
- 1 tsp. onion powder
- 1 tsp. red pepper, finely crushed
- 1 tsp. Worcestershire sauce

- 1 tsp. hot sauce
- 1 dash of cayenne pepper

Directions

1. Combine all ingredients in a large mixing bowl and whisk together until thoroughly combined. Whisk until all small clumps of seasonings are dissolved.
2. Pour into a container for serving and store in the refrigerator until ready to use.
3. You can use this sauce at the end of the cooking process on the grill or add it as it is plated as a condiment.

Note:

This recipe is heavy in mayonnaise content. Take care to keep it refrigerated until ready to use.

Poor Boy's Burnt Ends

Ingredients

- ➢ 1 chuck roast (at least 3" thick), 3-4 pounds
- ➢ 2 pinches Kosher salt
- ➢ 1 tbsp. garlic and pepper seasoning
- ➢ 1 tsp. onion powder
- ➢ 1 tsp. hot sauce
- ➢ 1 tsp. garlic sauce
- ➢ 1 tsp. Worcestershire sauce
- ➢ 1 tbsp. beef marinade
- ➢ 2 tbsp. smokey garlic and onion seasoning

- 1-1/2 cups barbecue sauce

Directions

1. Cut roast in half. Place roast on a cutting board and slice midway through the thickness of the roast as if you were butterflying a thick pork chop.
2. Take the two pieces of roast and apply a generous coating of Kosher salt to both sides.
3. Lightly sprinkle garlic and pepper seasoning and onion powder over the roast.
4. Drizzle one teaspoon of hot sauce and garlic sauce on each piece of roast.
5. Pour one teaspoon of Worcestershire sauce on each piece of roast.
6. Pour one tablespoon of your favorite beef marinade on each roast.
7. Rub all ingredients into the roast pieces and repeat on the opposite side of the meat.
8. Let set and marinate for thirty minutes while you get your smoker to temp 250 degrees.
9. Smoke at 250 degrees for two hours, remove, cut into small bite-size pieces, and place in an aluminum pan.
10. Lightly sprinkle smokey garlic and onion seasoning over beef chunks, mix well by hand, and repeat once more.
11. Pour half the barbecue sauce over the beef chunks, mix by hand, and repeat.

12. Continue to mix the sauce with the beef chunks until they are all covered.
13. Place back on a 250-degree smoker in the pan, uncovered for another hour, or until they are tender to your liking.

Poor Boy's Burnt Ends Grilled Cheese

Ingredients

- ➢ 1 chuck roast (at least 3" thick), 3-4 pounds
- ➢ 2 pinches Kosher salt
- ➢ 1 tbsp. garlic and pepper seasoning
- ➢ 1 tsp. onion powder
- ➢ 1 tsp. hot sauce
- ➢ 1 tsp. garlic sauce
- ➢ 1 tsp. Worcestershire sauce
- ➢ 1 tbsp. beef marinade
- ➢ 2 tbsp. smokey garlic and onion seasoning

- ➤ 1-1/2 cups barbecue sauce
- ➤ bread, thick sliced
- ➤ 8 oz. unsalted butter
- ➤ 1 tbsp. garlic, minced
- ➤ Provolone cheese, sliced
- ➤ smoked Gouda cheese, sliced

Directions for Burnt Ends

1. Cut roast in half. Place roast on a cutting board and slice midway through the thickness of the roast as if you were butterflying a thick pork chop.
2. Take the two pieces of roast and apply a generous coating of Kosher salt to both sides.
3. Lightly sprinkle garlic and pepper seasoning and onion powder over roast.
4. Drizzle one teaspoon of hot sauce and garlic sauce on each piece of roast.
5. Pour one teaspoon of Worcestershire sauce on each piece of roast.
6. Pour one tablespoon of your favorite beef marinade on each roast.
7. Rub all ingredients into the roast pieces and repeat on the opposite side of the meat.
8. Let set and marinate for thirty minutes while you get your smoker to temp 250 degrees.
9. Smoke at 250 degrees for two hours, remove, cut into small bite-size pieces, and plan in an aluminum pan.

10. Lightly sprinkle smokey garlic and onion seasoning over beef chunks, mix well by hand, and repeat once more.
11. Pour half the barbecue sauce over the beef chunks, mix by hand, and repeat.
12. Mix the sauce with the beef chunks until they are covered.
13. Place back on a 250-degree smoker in the pan, uncovered for another hour or until they are tender to your liking.

Directions for Grilled Cheese

1. Preheat the lightly oiled griddle surface on medium-high heat.
2. Melt butter and add minced garlic.
3. Using a pastry brush, spread garlic butter on one side of the bread.
4. Place buttered side down on the griddle.
5. Spread garlic butter on the opposite side of the bread you have placed on the griddle.
6. Place one slice of provolone cheese onto the bread.
7. Place one or two scoops of burnt ends onto the cheese.
8. Place another slice of bread butter side down onto the griddle.
9. Place one slice of smoked gouda cheese onto that slice.
10. Wait approximately sixty seconds, then scoop bread with sliced gouda off the griddle and place cheese side down onto bread slice with burnt ends.
11. Scoop the entire cheese sandwich up with a spatula and flip over onto the grill for another forty-five to sixty seconds.
12. Remove from the griddle, plate, and enjoy.

Smoked B & B Burgers (Bacon & Blue Cheese)

Ingredients

- 5 lbs. ground chuck
- 3 eggs
- 1/2 cup breadcrumbs
- 1/4 cup of your favorite beef dry seasoning
- 2 tbsp. marinade
- 2 tbsp. Worcestershire
- cooked bacon, chopped
- blue cheese, crumbled

Directions

1. Mix ground chuck with eggs, breadcrumbs, beef seasoning, marinade, and Worcestershire sauce.
2. Mix well by hand until all ingredients are blended into the meat.
3. Pinch off about a "tennis ball" size of ground chuck and form into a patty.
4. Press a small indention in the center of the burger. You might use the length of your index finger for this or something similar in size. You are merely making a bed for your stuffing.
5. Place bacon pieces and blue cheese into the indention. Be a little generous with these portions.
6. Fold the patty over the stuffing and reform it into a patty pressing the edges a bit to ensure the stuffing is secure in the middle.
7. Place on a pan and sprinkle a little more dry seasoning over the top of the burger.
8. Continue this until you use all the ground chuck. (When I created this recipe, I ended up with twelve hearty burger patties.)
9. Cover sheet pan of burgers with foil and place in the refrigerator.
10. Preheat the smoker to 275 degrees. I like to use light smoking wood such as pecan or maple for this smoke. We are looking for a gentle smoke taste and want to avoid using a stronger smoke such as mesquite or hickory.
11. Place burgers in the smoker and smoke until the internal temp is 160 degrees.
12. Remove and rest for a few minutes (Five minutes or so will suffice.) while you dress the buns.

13. You may consider toasting your burger buns in the oven for a bit.
14. Dress your burger buns with blue cheese dressing (see our recipe for homemade blue cheese dressing or use your favorite store-bought), sliced tomato, and a couple of pieces of cooked bacon.
15. Plate it, cut it in half, and serve.

Stuffed Smoked Meatloaf

Ingredients

- 4 lbs. ground beef
- 1 lb. fresh ground Cajun pork sausage
- 1/2 lb. cooked bacon
- 1 8 oz. package of cream cheese
- 1 8 oz. block of sharp cheddar cheese
- 1 cup burger marinade
- 1/4 cup garlic and onion seasoning (smoked/roasted flavor)
- 1 tbsp. hot sauce
- 3 cloves garlic
- 1 onion, loosely sliced
- Creole seasoning or favorite burger seasoning

Directions

1. In a large bowl, combine ground meat, marinade, garlic and onion seasoning, hot sauce, garlic, and onions and mix well by hand.
2. Flatten out on the countertop and spread evenly until the meat is about half an inch thick all the way around.
3. Lightly sprinkle Creole seasoning over the meat.
4. Cut cream cheese into strips and place down the center of the meat.
5. Roll Cajun sausage into a log just a bit shorter than the width of the ground meat and lay it on top of the cream cheese, then flatten it out a bit.
6. Cut the block of cheddar cheese into strips as we did for the cream cheese and place it on top of the sausage layer.
7. Finish off the stuffing by adding the strips of cooked bacon slices and laying them on top of the cheddar.
8. Roll both sides of the meatloaf up and over the stuffing layer.

Note: I have found it helpful to use a spatula to help with this. Simply slide a spatula under the loaf, lift and repeat down the entire length.

9. Pat the seams and ends into the loaf, ensuring we seal them well.
10. Generously sprinkle Creole seasoning or your favorite burger seasoning over the entire loaf and let it sit for about thirty minutes while your smoker gets to temp. We are looking for 275 degrees on our smoker.
11. Place loaf on the smoker and 275 degrees for approximately three

hours, or the internal temp is 160.

Tip: Place the loaf on a flat-edged pan so when it comes time to place it on the smoker, you can slide it off the pan by pushing it with the edges of another pan or a large spatula so the loaf does not break.

12. Remove from the smoker, set for five to ten minutes, slice it up and enjoy.

Note: Don't be afraid to experiment with your stuffing. Remember, recipes are only a guide. Make them your own by adjusting ingredients, changing some, and putting your signature on them.

Smoked Split Chicken with Alabama White Sauce

Ingredients

- 4 chicken halves, split
- roasted garlic avocado oil
- poultry rub
- garlic sauce marinade

Directions

1. Clean chicken halves under cool water, then pat dry with paper

towels
2. Lay chicken out on a pan and rub roasted garlic avocado oil on both sides of the chicken.
3. Sprinkle lightly with poultry rub
4. Lightly pour a small amount of garlic sauce marinade over the chicken and rub all over until there is a light coat of marinade over the entire chicken.
5. Generously sprinkle your favorite poultry rub on both sides of the chicken, the underside first, and the skin side second. This will assist in great flavor throughout.
6. Place in the fridge for thirty to forty-five minutes to allow the marinade to flavor the chicken.
7. Prep smoker to a temp of 275-300 degrees.
8. Place chicken on the smoker and cook for approx. Two and a half hours or until internal temperature reaches 165 degrees.
9. Once chicken hits the 165-degree mark, if you prefer, you might pour a little BBQ sauce over it and leave it on the smoker for another ten minutes (see the recipe in this book for Alabama White Sauce that I've found works well with chicken).
10. Remove from the smoker and serve.

Note:

Remember, it is essential to ensure chicken is thoroughly cooked. As stated in the recipe, you are looking for 165 degrees internal temperature. Another method is to grab the chicken leg, which is done if it moves about freely at the joint.

Be a Good Neighbor; It's Contagious

For the law if fulfilled in one word, even in this: "You shall love your neighbor as yourself." Galatians 5:14

Have you ever been part of something unintentional and been blown away by the results as you look back after the fact? This is my recollection of just one of the times we have witnessed this, and we often look at it as a perfect example of just doing something from the heart to help a neighbor or even someone that doesn't necessarily live next door and watch God work. God's Word tells us to "be kind to one another" in Ephesians 4:32. Acts of kindness can range from just the tiniest thing, such as a quick smile and brief "Hello," to larger things, such as buying someone groceries and delivering them or anything in between.

My wife, Michelle, and I bought a nice little house in a new subdivision, and we were excited! We moved in and soon began meeting our neighbors. Greg and Ebony lived directly next door, and as time passed, we had many conversations. We immediately took a liking to them and would always speak or wave if we saw them outside. Through our conversations, we learned that Greg and Ebony suffered from kidney disease and were on dialysis. I noticed that the first summer, they had someone coming every couple of weeks to cut their lawn and always kept it up nicely. I spend much time outside keeping my yard up and doing what I call piddling. I just tinker with things outside, listen to my music, work on small projects, and enjoy myself. I also find it's a great way to meet people. They're generally not going to come knocking on your door and say, "Hello, my name is…" fill in the blank. If you're outside and willing to engage, you can meet some awfully good folks, and Greg and Ebony are good folks.

As time passed, I noticed their lawn guy wasn't coming around anymore. I also realized that neither could get out and take care of their lawn. So, I began to cut their yard every other time I cut my own. I don't say this to brag and bring credit to myself at all. Please know that even though I'm an extrovert, often loud, and, as my wife says, never meet a stranger, I consider myself a very humble guy. I never went to my neighbors and asked permission or anything in return and never held any ill feelings toward them. I just wanted to help.

This went on for the entire year, and as the next grass-cutting season came around, something cool happened. One day I was about to cut my yard, and I looked next door and someone had already cut theirs. I didn't think much about it and thought it nice that they got their lawn taken care of. A couple of weeks later, I saw another neighbor come across the street with his mower, cutting their yard for them. So, between us, Greg and Ebony never once had to pay for someone to cut and trim their yard. As neighbors meet and see needs, they are moved to help meet those needs! Another need was their front flower bed. One day I got home from work, yet another neighbor was taking care of their flower bed. And another one came from down the street to help as well. The generosity and love shown from neighbor to neighbor was contagious and spreading like wildfire! Yes, the entire small section of our neighborhood eventually adopted this fine young couple and helped often. Greg and Ebony were very appreciative and smiling as they enjoyed life together. People helping people is just a great way of life, and all a fire of servanthood needs is a spark and a little wind to help it along. Soon after that initial spark, the fire spreads rampantly and makes an impact.

Our next-door neighbors no longer live here, as Ebony has since passed away, and Greg has also moved. I think of them often, and what a joy it was to serve them and watch a small community catch the spirit of kindness and being nice to our neighbors grew as contagious as the common cold.

You see, friends, we are called to serve. We are equipped to serve. We all have a specific talent, skill, and desire we can use to make a positive Kingdom impact in our circle of influence. I like to call that circle of influence our impact zone. I believe God placed Michelle and me next door to Greg and Ebony for a reason. I didn't know it then, but as I reflect on the past couple of years and think about how serving our neighbors became second nature, I see how God is constantly equipping us for his service. Through our serving together, God has allowed our neighborhood to become closer and more readily serve each other, which you will read in another story of how we band together, especially in the tough times.

I wish that as you read this, and other stories like it, you are inspired to make a difference in your impact zone and be moved to action. We can all affect someone's life through small acts of kindness.

Making a Difference and Impacting our Impact Zone

Therefore comfort each other and edify one another just as you also are doing.

1 Thessalonians 5:11

Have you ever considered the impact you are making and how the things we do or say can have far-reaching effects? It's been said that when you toss a pebble into a lake, the ripples continue until you can no longer see them. Let's take a little bit closer look at how we can make an impact in our impact zone and see if we can be reminded of just how large our impact zone is!

Pam Tebow wrote a book entitled "Ripple Effects,"[1] and she describes such a phenomenon in her writing. Ripple effects are an exciting concept that, as we examine, we will surely see the continuous and far-reaching impacts. Let's look at an example that happened to me.

In this example, we will see it's basically about transferring knowledge that we have gained to someone else, who passes that on to another person who also does the same. When I was a junior in high school playing baseball, we had a new coach come onto the staff. Coach Sid took our team when we began practice that year and told us we were returning to the fundamentals. He took the time to teach us proper techniques and fundamentals on throwing, fielding, and hitting. He began his instruction without even using a baseball. We didn't even touch a baseball, as I remember, for weeks. Everything we did focused on mechanics and fundamentals. We worked on our footwork, arm position, stance, how to run, slide, and better run bases. Coach took us and started from scratch. Once we added the actual baseball into the equation, we showed a dramatic improvement in our skills, which improved our team and transferred that improvement into wins on the baseball diamond. We were doubtful at first and didn't understand what was going on, but we had to follow along because he was the coach, and we were the players.

As I grew older and began to work with my children and help coach them, I always remembered what Coach Sid taught us and how important fundamentals were. I used this concept, although not to the degree that he did, but still used what had taught me at age seventeen and transferred much of the same instruction to our young teams, encouraging and coaching them to pay attention to the fundamentals. I now have two sons who have made a career in the teaching and coaching profession that do the same. What Coach Sid put in motion back in 1980 has been transferred generationally and will continue infinitely. If we asked him, coach would probably say he didn't just come up with this on his own and someone else had passed this on to him. That's how ripple effects work!

We have no idea our reach with the things we do and say. We all have an impact zone that expands beyond what we can even fathom. Another example of ripple effects we create is the things we say. As I shared in my first book, *Inspired Cooking*, in the story titled "The Words We Say" I share an example of how our words impact us. We all have that impact zone. The words we use, positive or negative, have ripple effects. For instance, when a child hears the words "You're a bad boy," "You're so stupid," and "You'll never amount to anything," that seed is planted in them. They will eventually transfer the same type of words. This ripple effect gives an example of negativity and the negative impacts it can have. You can easily see how damaging it is for a child to hear this message consistently. This is what they know, what they've been taught, and what they have in their tool bag, so this will be passed on. When we replace this source of negativity and replace it with affirming words such as "You are amazing," "You are a winner," "You are so worthy," and "You matter," we are setting the table and equipping that same child with a winning attitude. We are setting them up for success. We are setting those he meets years later for success. We are putting into motion something that can truly be impactful for generations to come. If you want to change the world, you can do it, one person at a time. There's a saying I've heard, and you may have heard it also referring to how you eat a burger—one bite at a time. When we bite into a burger, we only bite what we can handle. We cannot take the entire burger into our mouths and consume it. As such, we cannot take an entire community and change it overnight. We must focus on what we can chew on. We must focus on the small bites and make our impact right before us. The burger we are biting into and impacting is a small piece of our impact zone. We have the opportunity every day to create long-lasting ripple effects.

We were created for a purpose. Each of us has been given a special set of skills, abilities, and gifts to make an impact in our impact zone and set in motion a ripple effect that can and will change our world. Yes, you are an incredible human being with an incredible gift! You have capabilities that you cannot even fathom! You have a circle of influence that nobody else can reach. You have an impact zone that I don't have, and I have one that you don't have. Consider the possibilities of all the ripple effects put into motion daily! Every day, ripple effects are being sent out! Every day, we contribute to someone! Every day we have a chance to make an impact! Every day we have a choice about what impact we want to make. If we are intentional about positively impacting someone and set out to do just that, we can and will change our world for the better.

You see, you or I can make a difference! It's not out of the realm of possibility to one day get a phone call from someone you impacted with a voice on the other end saying, "Thank you." "Thank you for being such a positive influence in my life." "Thank you for believing in me." "Thank you for loving me." It can and does happen often. Every day, someone is being impacted and encouraged to be the best version of themselves God has created them to be. Every day we can speak life into someone and change the course of their day. Friends, we all have our impact zone and our ripple effects we start. I encourage you to be that positive change, that positive example, that light that shows someone they can and will! You can make a difference; you can be that positive impact in your impact zone, and I truly believe you will! I pray these words inspire you and possibly even bring someone to mind that you can reach out to right now and speak life into! Give that person a call, send them a text, reach out to them and let them know you care and believe in them! Do it right now! Let's all go out and make a difference today!

After the Storms

My little children, let us not love in word or tongue, but with deed and in truth. 1 John 3:18

June first through November thirtieth each year is a season for people living in states bordering the Gulf of Mexico is a season that can sometimes last for what seems like forever. Hurricane season in Louisiana is a season that is as unwelcome as a thief in the night. It is a season that, for six months, keeps residents alert with an eye on the tropics. A season that forces the citizenry to prepare for the worst and pray for the best. In 2020 and 2021, the entire state of Louisiana and our neighboring states felt the wrath and fury of this annual season like none other. Our state faced five named storms in 2020: Tropical Storms Cristobal and Marco, followed by Hurricanes Laura (Category 4), Delta, and Zeta. 2021 brought Hurricane Ida (Category 4) and Tropical Storm Claudette. A state known for southern hospitality, comfort food, and letting the good times roll was beaten down by unwelcome guests that left a mark of demolition, devastation, and destruction in its wake. Through these times of storms and crisis, we witness extraordinary acts of kindness and people that reach out and love with their actions and words.

I was blessed to be part of efforts after Hurricane Laura crippled Southwest Louisiana in 2020 and again after Hurricane Ida, the eye passing within twenty-five miles of my own house in 2021. Indeed, in times of crisis, God's provision shines. I would like to share with you a few stories of promise, a few stories of love, a few stories of compassion, and provision during a time of need and chaos.

Louisiana is no stranger to these types of storms. Over the years, named storms such as Andrew, Betsy, Camille, Katrina, Laura, Ida, and many others have left their mark on its people. After these vicious storms depart, their opportunities to help, serve, and meet needs are unlike any other time. I am grateful to have been spared major damage to my property and life so that I might be able to go out and serve my neighbors while being the hands and feet of Jesus.

Hurricane Laura, as I mentioned, came ashore in Southwest Louisiana, devastating everything in its path. Power lines were mangled, roofs gone, trees blown down onto homes and businesses, and small towns completely erased any structures. One of my sons and his family live in Southwest Louisiana, and as his home was, for the most part, spared, many surrounding him were not. We partnered up with a group of young people in The Fellowship of Christian Athletes along with my other children, and a few friends drove the three-hour drive to get there, and what we witnessed was powerful. We saw strangers helping strangers, cutting downed trees, and helping residents pick up the pieces of their lives and stack them on the curb.

We witnessed families helping families, unconcerned about who they were, what they looked like, or how they spoke. What we witnessed and were a part of was a massive act of humanity being performed by people that whether they knew it or not, were doing God's work. These are the times when people shine. These are the times when we come together for a common purpose and the greater good. We were able to help not only my son but a couple of his neighbors as well. One lady lived across the street from my son David. She was a single mom with a couple of children, and they were all out working alongside us as we cut up a fallen tree that had just missed her house. We had a chance to pray with her as we wrapped things up and provided some additional water and food before we left. She cried, we cried, and shared sweaty hugs as we left to help another neighbor.

Then we met a seventy-eight-year-old marine and his wife who had been working and trying to do what they could to pick things up and get some sense of normalcy. The stories he shared and his gratitude for helping them, even though we had never met, restored faith in mankind that day. His wife insisted we eat with them as another group of volunteers was handing out hot meals. I remember sitting on their back porch, taking a break while we enjoyed some good company and a bowl of red beans and rice. What a joy to be able to help!

The next weekend, we returned with some more friends and fed 400 people a hot meal. The weekend after, two weeks after the storm, another group of our friends made the trip again and fed another 1000 people a hot spaghetti dinner! We have a saying that rings true, "People helping people, it's what we do." The most significant thing about these examples is that they are only a drop in the bucket of examples of generosity, selflessness, and servanthood. When these events happen, people show out!

Fast forward to 2022, and Southeast Louisiana faces the same thing a year later. Once again, we see God's provision at work. The weekend immediately following the storm, we partnered with a friend's church and went to Houma, Louisiana, with the intent to feed six hundred. When I speak on God's provision, hear me when I say that our God will and does provide. About twenty of us went down to Houma, set up our canopies, and began cooking. We were preparing sausage po'boys for six hundred of our neighbors whose entire area was demolished. We cooked the sausage on a thirty-six-inch Blackstone griddle and about the same size charcoal pit—six hundred sausage po'boys—but wait, there's more!

When we began serving the community, they brought more food for us to cook. It was incredible! They brought chicken, burgers, fish, frog legs; you name it, and they brought it. They were sending a message to us to say "thank you," and through that provision, we were able to feed an additional six hundred people! What a blessing and what an amazing day that was! We go there intending to feed six hundred, and God says, "Wait up, y'all! There's more for you to feed! There's enough for another six hundred! Now get busy!" So, we did. We got busy and stayed until the last of the twelve hundred meals were given out. Twelve hundred meals in four hours. What an unbelievable day, all because of God's provision and a willingness to put others before ourselves.

This type of work has grown into a passion, and I write this story not to boast about what we did but to boast about what God did. We serve a God of provision! When we surrender to His will, acknowledge who He is, and take that step of faith, God equips, guides, and provides. Storms are trying and scary, but remember, through the storm, on the other side of the storm are opportunities to grow and make an impact in your impact zone. Be bold enough to step out and make that impact and be amazed at what God can do through you!

What's Next?

When you have eaten and are full, then you shall bless the Lord your God for the good land which He has given you. Deuteronomy 8:10

Gratitude is such a crazy and powerful thing. I have found that if I am truly grateful for things and voice them consistently, I already have everything I need! You see, there's a difference between needs and wants. Here's an example: We need a roof over our heads, but we may want a roof covering a 3500-square-foot house. We need to be fed daily, but we may want prime rib even though we already have ground meat. There's nothing wrong with wanting and desiring more and seeking an increase. God will provide these wants as He sees fit. If we are responsible with what he has already given us, He will provide an increase.

Further, I believe we should guard our minds and spirit and ask for God's favor and protection as we increase. If we begin with a grateful heart, God will reveal what is to be next, our next move, whom we should impact next, and where we should focus our efforts next. Allow me to explain in a little more detail what I mean.

Two years ago, I was introduced to a social media group called #RiseandGrind. Its founder, Glenn Lundy, would say if you want to change the world, you must change how you start your day. Glenn is a strong advocate of getting up early, spending time in prayer, spending time in gratitude, spending time on your physical health, writing down your daily goals, and encouraging others. One thing I learned as I began to put this into action is that once I committed to having a grateful heart, it became easier for me to see and count all the blessings I already have and recognize and acknowledge where they came from. By doing so, I surrendered a mighty and powerful force, and I believe He wants his people to succeed. However, I also believe in humility and have experienced the great loss of things due to an ungrateful heart.

As I began daily committing to a heart of gratitude and giving God credit (like He needs it for Him to feel good), I began to see a shift in my mindset. It became clearer to me what direction God wanted me to move in, and it became clearer who I was meant to speak to and encourage that day or at that moment. It became clearer to me for my future. Through my gratefulness for the provision that I already had, I became responsible for more blessings, for which I am also truly grateful. Some examples are blessings of a great marriage, blessings of good health, blessings of many grandchildren, blessings of reliable vehicles, and blessings of a back porch patio cover that will soon be constructed. These are all blessings of God for which I am truly grateful.

I share this as an encouragement to you to begin your day in prayer and meditation, if only to test my ideas and see where it goes. As you begin each day, I encourage you to verbally express and even write down one or two things you are grateful for that day and truly be thankful for whatever it is. Once we focus on gratitude, it becomes much tougher to focus on negativity, what we don't have, or what we wish we had. A heart of gratitude goes a long way to mental, spiritual, and physical health. We begin to smile more, we begin to have more energy, we begin to want to pray more, and we begin to show how we feel to others.

Here are some practical ways to begin your day in gratitude:

1. Spend two minutes at the start of your day and list things for which you are grateful.

2. Verbalize your gratitude. Speak it out of your mouth and audibly say, "I am grateful for a new day. I am grateful for the rain, the sunshine, and the temperature. I am grateful today for the coffee I am drinking. I am grateful for the ability to feed my children. I am grateful for the person I'm going to meet today. Thank you for all the blessings."

3. Take a gratitude walk. Take time to get out, walk, pay attention to your surroundings, and express gratitude for that. Recently I was on a camping trip with my son and grandson. One morning, my grandson Cooper and I took a walk. As we walked around the campsite, I asked him to tell me one thing he was thankful for, and we took turns listing them. We got some physical exercise in, spent some quality time together, and Coop saw an example of what being thankful looks like. Honestly, I'm not sure who enjoyed it more, him or me, but I know I felt terrific afterward.

4. Throughout the day, take a brief gratitude inventory. You can do this in your mind, speak it, or write it down. I have found that doing this once or twice during the day helps reinforce my gratitude and helps keep negativity away.

5. Before you sleep, speak about what you are most grateful for today. Celebrate that gratitude, and as you doze off for a good

night's sleep, get ready to get up tomorrow morning in another day of gratitude.

Grateful thinking and a grateful mindset have allowed me to do things I never considered. As I am working on writing this second book and coaching another aspiring author along his journey, it is very apparent to me that without humble gratitude, this would not and could not be happening. I am grateful for the very words I get to put down on this page and grateful for each eye that reads them. I am grateful for just a small chance to make a kingdom impact. I am grateful for my readers and their support of my projects, and as I keep this attitude of gratitude in place and give that mindset priority, I cannot help but wonder what's next! I am truly grateful for whatever that might look like and welcome it with excitement and thankfulness. Be grateful, friends, and test this out; I think you'll be amazed.

10/10/80

Give, and it will be given to you: good measure, pressed down, shaken together, and running over will be put into your bosom. For with the same measure that you use, it will be measured back to you. Luke 6:38

A rule of life was recently shared with me a couple of years ago, and I would like to pass this on to you. The application of this rule has been instrumental in our life, and whether you believe in God or not, the impact you can make by applying this rule to your life has the potential to be huge. This rule is known as the 10/10/80 rule. It simply states that we should give ten percent of our income to God, put ten percent into our savings, and live on the other eighty percent.

I had always known of tithing ten percent and giving that back to God by financially supporting my local church. However, I was not dedicated to it. When times got tough and money got tight, the first thing I would cut would be my giving. I would automatically look there first, even though what I was giving wasn't even the ten percent we are speaking of, it didn't matter to me the scriptural basis of giving. What mattered was that this money was better in my pocket than the church. I needed this money to make ends meet. I had to have this money. This money is mine and was provided for me to pay my bills and support my family. I had a mindset of selfishness. My mindset was one of a hoarder. If I hid it, I would have it to do what I wanted.

There was a problem, however. Even though I tried to hide it away and put it up, I never had enough. I never had enough to do things I wanted, no matter how small they might have been. I was always in need. I felt I was always in search of. I felt financially inadequate.

Have you ever done things you know aren't right but still do it anyway? Maybe you feel like you know better. Maybe you feel like you want to be in control. Maybe you reject what has been said just out of spite; just because. Whatever the reason, I had been making the choice that ultimately had me being handcuffed to an unfulfilled life.

I'm a little unclear as to why I started to apply this principle to our spending habits. Maybe it was part of the growth journey I started back in 2018. Maybe it was a sermon I heard on a particular Sunday. Maybe it was something as simple as being sick and tired of being sick and tired and broke. Whatever pushed me to that point of trying to live by this rule, I can certainly say I am so glad I took that step. When we finally decide to accept the Word and live the life we can, great things happen. This is not to say that there will not be challenges and tough times. What happens is that we are equipped to handle these challenges.

Last year, I decided to go on my first-ever mission trip. By this point, I had been applying the 10/10/80 rule for a couple of years and had already seen evidence of what this principle could do. The cost of the trip was $750.00 per person. In my mind, I began to question whether I could afford to go or not. I kept trying to come up with other things to do with that money. Finally, I took the step of faith, paid my money, and said to myself, "God's got this." That afternoon our mail was delivered, and to my surprise, there was a check for $754.00 from an insurance policy for an overpayment we did not know of! Yes, our God does provide! Yes, our needs are met!

This type of faithful stewardship has happened time and time again, from large things to small things. From things that might seem insignificant at the time to things that seem life-changing, our needs are met, and we have been equipped to give from the overflow!

For a large part of my life, I had been a beneficiary of people's generosity. We had received gifts over the years from people that were giving from their overflow. When we began to apply this rule of life, we have now been able to give from the overflow as well! We have been able to build a small business that has primarily provided a vehicle to meet needs where they are. We were able to feed our small subdivision last year during the aftermath of Hurricane Ida. We have been able to sponsor children to attend youth camps at church. We have been able to support young student-athletes as they grow in their individual and team sports. We have also supported our community as we pay it forward and help the next generation become who they are.

By tithing our ten percent first to God, giving ourselves ten percent for our savings, and living on the rest, we have been able to fully understand what God's word means when we read passages of Scripture like Luke 6:38. The 10/10/80 rule, when applied, can and will be life-changing. It has created a new heart in me and within me a new desire and ability to serve.

I will tell you this. Our God equips us to do the great things we are destined to do. We were created for greatness and can make a positive impact in our impact zones. We can do this while struggling and wondering where our needs will be met or while giving from the overflow of His blessings. When we obey, freely commit, and choose to apply God's principles in our lives, we can do so much more! It is my prayer that as you read this story, you are spirit-led and encouraged to decide to apply this rule to your life and see what happens! If you do, you will be amazed at what can be done and the lives that will be impacted!

Breakfast Bowls

Ingredients

- 1 lb. ground breakfast sausage
- 6 ramekin bowls
- 6 large eggs
- 6 frozen biscuits
- dash of salt and pepper
- 6 tbsp. unsalted butter (one per ramekin)
- cheese, shredded

Directions

1. Preheat oven to 400 degrees
2. In a skillet, brown breakfast sausage and crumble it up as it cooks.
3. Remove from the skillet onto a paper towel-lined platter.
4. Cover the sausage with another layer of paper towels and press down with your hands to squeeze out as much excess grease as possible.
5. Spray the inside of each ramekin with cooking spray.
6. Place frozen biscuit in a ramekin.
7. Add about one-eighth of a cup of browned breakfast sausage, spreading over and around the biscuit.
8. Crack one egg into a separate bowl and scramble, then pour into a ramekin.
9. Sprinkle a dash of salt and pepper over the mixture.
10. Repeat this process for all six ramekins.
11. Place breakfast-filled ramekins onto a baking sheet, place in the oven, and bake for about twenty to twenty-five minutes. Bake until the tops of the biscuits are light brown and the egg has firmed up.
12. Remove from the oven. Place one tablespoon unsalted butter on top of the biscuit.
13. Add about one-third of a cup of your favorite shredded cheese.
14. Place back in the oven just long enough for the butter and cheese to melt.
15. Remove from the oven and let rest for five minutes.
16. Use a small plastic spatula to run along the sides of the ramekin and ensure it is completely separated from the contents.

17. Gently scoop out, plate, and serve.

Vacay Biscuits & Gravy

A very simple and easy breakfast to make on a family vacation and a crowd pleaser!

Ingredients

- ➤ 2 cans of already-made biscuits
- ➤ 2 packs of country gravy mix
- ➤ 1-1/2 lbs. of ground breakfast sausage

Directions

1. Follow the directions on the label for biscuits.
2. Brown breakfast sausage and crumble as it browns.

3. Follow directions on gravy packets.
4. Pour gravy over top of the sausage.
5. Let it set for just a bit, and it will thicken.
6. Serve up your family's breakfast and start your vacation day.

Crawfish Cheese Omelet

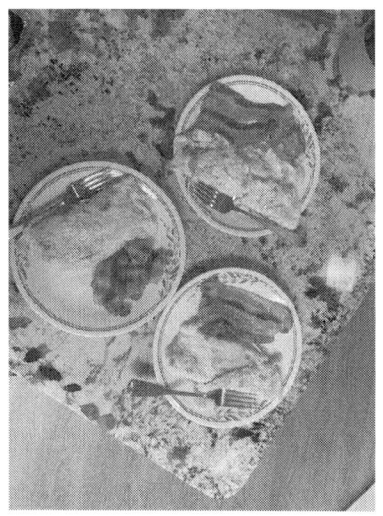

Ingredients

- 2 eggs
- 1 tbsp. whole milk
- 1/4 cup crawfish tails
- 1/8 cup cheese, shredded
- Pinch of salt
- Pinch of black pepper

Directions

1. In a small bowl, crack two eggs, and add milk, salt, and pepper.
2. Mix well and set to the side.

3. Preheat your nonstick skillet to medium temp.
4. Pour your eggs into the skillet.
5. Add crawfish and cheese down the center of the eggs.
6. When eggs begin to cook enough to flip, use a sturdy spatula and flip one side (one-third of the egg) over the top of the crawfish and cheese
7. Wait a couple of minutes and flip the other third of the egg over the top of the center.
8. Again, let it cook a couple more minutes and flip the entire omelet over for one more minute.
9. Remove and set on the serving plate.

Oven-Baked Cheesy-Meaty Breakfast

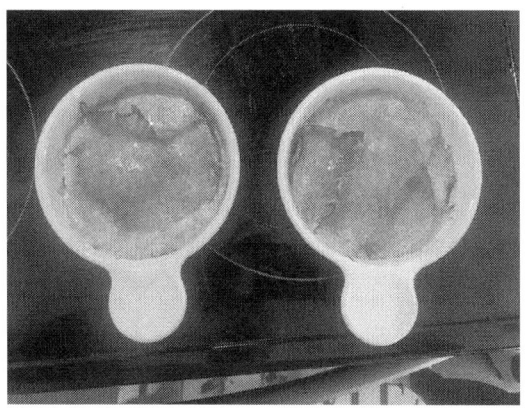

Ingredients Per Bowl

- ➢ 1 8 oz. oven-safe baking bowl
- ➢ 2 eggs (well-beaten)
- ➢ 1 pack of Hawaiian sweet rolls
- ➢ 1/4 cup smoked sausage, cut into bite-size chunks
- ➢ 1/4 cup Colby Jack cheese, grated
- ➢ 2 deli ham, thinly sliced
- ➢ Another 1/4 cup of Colby Jack cheese, grated
- ➢ 1 pat of unsalted butter
- ➢ salt and pepper to taste

Directions

1. Preheat oven to 350 degrees.

2. Spray the entire inside of a bowl with cooking spray.
3. Place the Hawaiian sweet roll in the center of the bowl.
4. Add smoked sausage chunks around the sweet roll.
5. Pour well-beaten egg over the top of the roll and sausage.
6. Sprinkle one-fourth of a cup of cheese over the mixture.
7. Place two slices of deli ham, covering the entire top of the ingredients.
8. Place bowl in 350-degree preheated oven.
9. Bake for twenty minutes.
10. Remove from the oven.
11. Add the last one-fourth of a cup of cheese on top of the ham.
12. Return to the oven for five minutes.
13. **Remove from the oven, and let cool for five to ten minutes before serving, as the bowl is extremely hot!**

Mama G's Crawfish Pie
Via Ruth Glaser Watts

Ingredients

- 1 cup finely chopped onions
- 1 stick butter
- 1 lb. Louisiana crawfish tails
- 1/4 cup chopped or finely sliced green onion tops
- 1 10.5 oz. can cream of mushroom soup
- 1 tbsp. cornstarch
- 1 5 oz. can evaporated milk
- 3/4 tsp. salt
- 3/4 tsp. white pepper

➢ 2 nine-inch-deep dish pie shells

Directions

1. Preheat oven to 350 degrees.
2. Sauté chopped onions in melted butter until they are clear.
3. Check peeled crawfish tails for shell pieces, and gently rinse under cool water.
4. Drain water off tails spread thinly on a paper towel-lined pan. Cover crawfish with a paper towel and pat dry.
5. Add green onions and crawfish tails to sautéed onions, stir, cover, and place heat on low. Cook on low heat for twenty to twenty-five minutes.
6. Add cream of mushroom soup. (Do not dilute).
7. Add salt and white pepper.
8. Dilute cornstarch in evaporated milk and add to the crawfish mixture.
9. Allow coming to a full boil, constantly stirring to prevent sticking.
10. Remove from heat and allow to cool.
11. Fill the pie shell with the mixture and add the other pie shell on top.
12. Place pie on a baking pan and bake for 25-30 minutes or until the crust is golden brown.
13. Remove from the oven, let set for a while, slice, serve, and enjoy!

Special Diet Information

Some people have severe allergies to shellfish or shellfish products. Please understand that crawfish are shellfish and could trigger an allergic reaction.

Granny Ruth's Crawfish Etouffee
Via Ruth Glaser Watts

Ingredients

- 2 lbs. Louisiana peeled crawfish tails, cleaned
- 1/2 lb. (2 sticks of butter)
- 2 medium onions, chopped
- 1 large green bell pepper, chopped
- 1 medium red bell pepper, chopped
- 2 ribs celery, chopped
- 1/2 cup Italian parsley, chopped
- 1/2 cup green onion tops, chopped or thinly sliced
- 2 small pods of garlic, finely minced
- salt, pepper, and Creole seasoning to taste
- 2 tsp. paprika

- ➢ 2 cans of golden mushroom soup
- ➢ 2 heaping tbsps. cornstarch (mixed in ½ cup water)

Directions

1. Sauté onion, peppers, celery, and garlic into melted butter until soft. DO NOT BROWN.
2. Add the golden mushroom soup, stirring well.
3. Add the cleaned crawfish tails with all their fat.
4. Add the seasonings and cover the pot over low heat to smother the crawfish etouffee until tails are cooked, twelve to fifteen minutes.
5. Stir in paprika, parsley, and green onion tops.
6. Stir the cornstarch into the water in a separate bowl, then add to etouffee, constantly stirring so it does not clump.
7. Cook on low heat for about six minutes.

Note: Thicken sauce to adhere to the rice.

8. Serve over cooked long grain rice.
9. This recipe serves six to eight.

Sidenote: This recipe is one that Granny Ruth's granddaughter, my niece Britney, asked her to cook for her and Matt and her wedding reception.

Mom – What a Woman!

And he went and got them and brought them to his mother, and his mother made savory food, such as his father loved. Genesis 27:14

One thing I have learned over the years is this: Mothers, moms, mamas, or whatever you might call yours, are a very special part of our lives. My mom was just that. She was special. As I reflect on her impact on me, I am reminded of just what a strong woman she was.

Patricia Ann Pittman was born on February 15, 1941, and was the only daughter of four children to Cecil and Marie Pittman. She grew up in what is affectionately called "the parish" by locals in New Orleans in the community of Chalmette. I don't quite recall how she met my dad, but I know they married young and began living together in New Orleans, where they lived until 1965 when Hurricane Betsy came ashore and flooded them out. At that time, she was pregnant with my sister, Donna, and I remember the story she told me about that night. As she recalled, the storm was coming in with lots and lots of rain, and streets began taking on water.

As you may be aware, the city of New Orleans rests below sea level and is prone even to flash flooding, which is why the city now has a series of pumps staged throughout that the people of New Orleans heavily rely on. Mom told me this story many times as other storms came our way. I believe it was her way of resting her soul, as I'm sure her anxiety level would elevate every time a storm was in the Gulf of Mexico. She spoke of her dad sitting in the living room, hearing the howling wind and monitoring the rising water. I remember the crazy part of this story: When they saw the coffee table begin to rise and fall as the floor of their elevated home began to rise and fall along with the water. It was then; dad decided it was time to go. They grabbed what they could, and with a one and half-year-old and a pregnant wife in tow, dad got us all to safety, and at that moment, we were now classified as survivors of one of the most horrific hurricanes to make landfall in the United States at that time.

Showing true resiliency, mom would work hard to put pieces of our life back together, and we moved a little further to the north across Lake Pontchartrain, where her mom and dad lived. Folsom, Louisiana, is where mom and dad raised me in my early years as a child until later, we would move once more to Baton Rouge. I can remember these five years when I saw my mom work as a quote "homemaker," which was typical of the era in American history. Mom worked on taking care of the home, and dad went to work every day to provide financially as best he could. Mom was a very patient woman, especially with me.

When I was a child, I tended to want to push buttons, and I would antagonize her and push her as far as I could. I loved my mom, but I just had a streak in me that I hope no mother ever must deal with. I would push her to her limits of patience, and then she would let me have it. I would hear the words "Wait till your dad gets home." frequently, and when dad would come home and mom would spill the beans on my behavior, I would pay the price of my antagonism and desire to stir the pot. I remember a particular instance when we were in the kitchen, and I was being my usual pain in the butt. Once again, I pushed her to her patience to the end, and the next thing I knew, a can of soup was landing loudly against the wall behind me! I was like, whoa! I started crying, and she was crying. I told her I was sorry, we hugged, made up, and everything was fine.

My mom didn't even have a driver's license until after I graduated high school. If any driving was going to happen, it was my dad's responsibility. I'm not sure if this was a "dad" thing or yet another thing of the era, but I'm assuming this was another typical thing of the times. I know that I had my driver's license before she did; once that happened, I could drive her to the grocery and stuff. We had moved to Baton Rouge by this time, and it was here that the rest of my childhood was lived out under the watchful care and support of my mom. She was always there for me, knew the right things to say, encouraged me, and showed her love for me.

Mom worked very hard in our home, raising her now four children: My sister Donna, our youngest twin brother and sister, Dale and Dawn, and myself. On top of being one of the hardest working and loving moms on the planet, she was also a devout wife who lived to please her husband. I can remember her having a pot of fresh coffee made for dad when he would get home in the evening, supper ready and waiting, and when he came home, she doted after him and did her best to care for him as well. My mom worked her tail off to be the best wife and mother she could be. I remember her asking for rides from friends to go to the grocery store or make doctor visits when we were sick. I remember her making sure I had transportation to baseball and football practices. I also remember walking home after many of them, which I didn't mind unless it was raining. I remember her walking to the corner store or asking one of us to go to the store and pick up a missing ingredient for what she was cooking. Looking back, I can't wrap my head around her inability to drive.

In 1982, when I graduated high school, her life was turned upside down. She and dad were on the outs, and dad had moved out. He would come by from time to time and visit, but he had effectively removed himself from the family. In May of that year, just nine days before I was to graduate high school, there was a knock on our door early one Saturday morning. I went to the door. Standing outside were two men dressed in suits, and one was holding a copy of my dad's driver's license. They asked me to speak to my mother. She got up, put on her robe, and as I stood next to her, my mom received the horrific news that dad had committed suicide. I had to catch her as her knees buckled, and she began to sob. I held her and tried to be as strong as I could for my mom. I was in shock; my younger siblings were waking up, and our world as we knew it was now nothing like we knew it. Through the love and support of family and friends, my mom moved forward and raised all her children as best she could. She got her license, got a job, bought a house, and pinched and saved and squeezed everything she could out of a dollar. She was there for me when I graduated from basic training. She was there for me when I got married. She was there for me whenever I needed to hear her voice or needed an ear. She was there for me during my divorce. She was there for me until the very end.

Mom always put her children's needs in front of her own. She was a mother who loved us unconditionally, parented us as best she could, provided for us to the best of her ability, and listened to us when we needed her. She was the ultimate mother and truly lived her life for each of us.

We lost my mom in 2016 after her battle with pancreatic cancer. I was living in North Mississippi at the time. My wife, Michelle, was here in Baton Rouge. She was able to spend some time with her mom. I had just finished working a night shift at the mill, and Michelle called me to say she thought I needed to come home; mom was not doing well. Her voice told me that this was a matter of grave importance. I told her I would nap for a couple of hours, get on the road, and call her. I was probably about fifty miles into a 380-mile trip when Michelle told me the news. Mom had gone home to be with Jesus—no more pain, no more hurt, nothing but peace and happiness. Michelle and my siblings were able to be with her until the end, and the nursing home kept mom there until I could get there a few hours later for me to see her. I cried the entire way there. The woman who loved me more than anyone ever was now not here. She was my rock, my confidant, and my biggest supporter. I miss her dearly to this very day and still have her number saved on my phone.

I pray that your relationship with your mom is cherished. We only have one mother, and I pray that if your relationship is not what it could be, you might be able to begin a restoration process that will move your mother-to-child relationship to a loving and positive level. We are not guaranteed tomorrow. We don't know what tomorrow will bring. Please don't wait. If there are fences that need to be mended, get your hammer and nails out and start mending. You can do it. God can help you. Commit to prayer, let God equip you, and rekindle that relationship. If you and your mother are on great terms, celebrate that greatness and enjoy each other's love! Enjoy each passing moment!

Sunshine

Every good gift and every perfect gift is from above, and comes down from the Father of lights, with whom there is no variation or shadow of turning. James 1:17

Allow me to introduce you to my daughter Abby. Abigail Grace is our fifth child, the only daughter my first wife and I have, and she was a miracle! Appropriately, her name in Hebrew means "my Father's Joy."[2] After four rough and tumble boys, my wife at the time, Shirley, and I wanted so much to have a daughter. After three miscarriages, we had given up hope when we got the news that she was, indeed, pregnant. I remember we held our excitement close to the vest as we moved through the first trimester. You see, we had learned that, for some reason, the three miscarriages that had occurred during that first three months were probably a girl, and we anxiously looked forward to getting past that point. It seemed that we were subconsciously expecting the worst every day and were surprised and relieved to get past the roadblock we had finally fallen apart on three times prior. However, as this turned out, we had agreed this would be our last attempt, and thankfully we were blessed with a beautiful baby girl!

Abby is truly a ray of sunshine for me and a learning experience. Unbeknownst to her, she taught me to be gentler in voice, spirit, and action. I can remember being quite protective of her with the boys, who often caught my wrath and sadly were the target of my anger and frustration. I was new to this game of being a daughter-dad and had a lot to learn. Here I was, allowed to receive this wonderful gift from God, and I was unprepared and felt unequipped to handle daughter-daddy. All I knew was that I loved this little girl with all my inner being and worshiped the ground her little feet walked on.

Abby and I would sit together and sing to her, which I didn't do with her brothers. This was her special time with me and my special time with her. I made up a song, and it went like this:

> Sunshine, Abby's daddy's sunshine
> Sunshine, Abby's daddy's sunshine
> She smiles, and the whole world smiles too
> Sunshine, Abby's daddy's sunshine
> Sunshine, Abby's daddy's sunshine
> She smiles and says I love you too
> Sunshine, Abby's daddy's sunshine
> Sunshine, Abby's daddy's sunshine
> I smile and say I love you too because
> Sunshine, Abby's daddy's sunshine

We would sit and sing that song together, and I remember it being such a special time. A time that it seemed nothing else mattered that was going on; nothing else really existed. There's something to be said for a daddy-and-daughter relationship.

Within a couple of years after her birth, Abby began having some health complications. She complained of aching legs and painful joints. Shirley brought her to the doctor, and a series of tests were run, and we found they suspected her of having this ailment called JDMS Juvenile Dermatomyositis, which causes muscle weakness, skin rash, and inflammation of the blood vessels, muscles, and skin. It about 3,000-5,000 kids in the United States, most between the ages of five and ten.[3] Her mother and I were gut-punched and felt blindsided. How could this be? Why is this happening to our precious daughter? How can I make it go away? Why? Just why? After shedding many tears and leaning on each other, we brought Abby in for a biopsy, where it was confirmed that Abby had this rare childhood disease. We had to protect her from the sun, as she would develop a serious rash and her muscles and joints ached all the time. Fortunately, she outgrew this disease, thriving at McNeese State University and living her best life!

Abby and I have not always had the greatest relationship and have not been as close as I envisioned. Truthfully, it's my doings. When she was 8, I stepped away from my marriage to Shirley and suffered the fate of having a distant relationship with my sunshine. It pains me to know that I hurt my daughter so much with the decisions I made, and I am writing this to encourage other dads and daughters that this can be overcome. However, it can only be overcome through reconciliation. First, I had to own my decision and make peace with my God.

You see, God can and will truly restore things. He's in the business of healing relationships, bodies, and illnesses. He's also in the business of forgiving. God's Word tells us that when we confess our sins, we are forgiven and cleansed (1 John 1:9). So, eight years after I left, I brought this burden to the only place I knew and left it there. I laid it at the feet of the cross, asked for forgiveness, and prayed for reconciliation to my children, especially my younger ones, Abby included. When I did that, magical things began to happen! I reached out to my children and told them what I had done, and little did I realize that God had also been working on their hearts. He had also sent them urges and messages to forgive and confess. That was nearly three years ago, and although things are not perfect, they have gotten much better. Just two days ago, Abby texted me asking for my advice and input on a decision she was dealing with on whether to go on a mission trip or not.

So you see, we cannot do things with our strength. When we try to take control, we will surely not be as successful as we could be by relying on God's strength. God blessed us with a wonderful daughter, and even though our relationship was severed, He restored it and is mending it daily! I hope this story about my Sunshine adds a little sunshine to your day and encourages you to maybe reconcile a damaged relationship by bringing it to the greatest healer there ever was and remains today! It won't be a cakewalk by any means, but I can tell you it will be worth it! Abby, you remain my sunshine, and I love you dearly. I know our God has big plans for us, and life is much better with you!

Friends, as you read these short stories, I pray you are somehow encouraged by my transparency to mend some fences you need to mend. As you continue in this book, you will be introduced to several of my other children and how God has also restored those relationships.

This Isn't an All-You-Can-Eat-Place!

And God is able to make all grace abound toward you, that you, always having all sufficiency in all things, may have an abundance for every good work. 2 Corinthians 9:8

Our weekends were spent mostly on the road when our boys played travel baseball. As shared in the story "God's Timing," we created many memories while traveling in my first book. One such memory that comes to mind is a weekend baseball tournament in New Orleans. My second oldest son, Zack, was playing this weekend, and if memory serves me correctly, our oldest son, David, was playing in Baton Rouge, so my wife and I decided to divide and conquer. She would stay in Baton Rouge with David and the younger boys, Gregg and Ryan, and Zack and I would go to New Orleans.

The trip from Central to New Orleans took about one and a half hours from the driveway to the parking lot, so we did not stay the night and travel back and forth to save the cost of hotel rooms. Zack and I were riding friends and road warriors for the weekend. We were also friends who loved to eat together too.

On Saturday, after we played and were on the way home, the discovery was made that Piccadilly, a restaurant chain that offered fresh, cafeteria-style food, is not an "all-you-can-eat deli." Knowing that we were both hungry, we decided to stop and grab a bite to eat before we headed home.

So, in we go to what Zack must have seen as the most awesome food-getting place in the world because as he walked down the serving line and passed in front of all of the many food options, he couldn't help but pick up everything he wanted to try; fried chicken, roast, potatoes, gravy, rolls, a couple of different deserts, and honestly, I can't remember all he put on his tray. And, being the dad that had a hard time telling my kids "no" to things, especially when it comes to food, I just let him roll with it and skimped back on my portions and selection to allow him to get what he wanted.

You see, things were always money tight for us. At that time, I was just starting a sales job, being allowed to prove myself after several years of warehouse work, truck driving, and warehouse leadership with a local company that sold plumbing supplies. My wife then worked as a childcare provider and focused on caring for our children. Even though our resources were limited, we could rob Peter to pay Paul, often going without, so our children go with. This weekend was one of those weekends for us. Enough of the back story; let's go back inside the Piccadilly and see how this story plays out!

At the end of the serving line, gathering all your food and setting plates, bowls, cups, and saucers of the bounty you've collected in what seemed to be an active twelve-year-old must be the greatest thing ever, waiting for the lady at the cash register. This cash register to a parent struggling to make ends meet and wanting to give his son the best experience he can has the appearance of something scary. Fear of the unknown creeps in. Fear of having to say "no" creeps in. Our parental fear kicks in that we might not have enough money as we try and prepare, in our minds, what our escape strategy is, or what our plan B is. It's like the furnace in the basement in the movie *Home Alone* that the main character, Kevin, sees and, in his mind, envisions a growling, snarling, gnashing of-teeth monster.[4] That is what I remember that cash register looking like.

As the lady began to enter purchase amounts for each item placed on our trays, from the largest item of fried chicken to the smallest item of a pat of butter and everything in between, the noise of the register calculating the cost grew louder and louder and louder. The roar became deafening, and my anxiety was growing to a capacity of complete stress. Thoughts were going through my mind at a pace so rapid that if it were an Indy race, there would have been no other driver that could keep up. The reality is that this was not an Indy race. This was true life. This was raising a family and trying our best with what we had. This was not wanting to have to say "no" to your child. This was a desire to give your child what he wanted. This was, in my mind, a chance for me to put my Superman cape on and be a hero to my son.

All these thoughts ran through my head in the short time the cashier took to tally up our bill. Fortunately, all my fears were false, and I had enough to pay for our meal. After we ate, my twelve-year-old, baseball-playing, normal little boy looked at me and said, "I thought this was an all-you-can-eat place." You see, I believe we both learned something that day. I learned that my son knew of my fears, and he understood based solely on his comments and actions based on his narrow window of what he could look through and see. And Zack learned his dad did have fears, as well as the revelation that Piccadilly Cafeterias are not an all-you-can-eat place!

As parents, we try to do our best for our children. We try to provide for them all their needs and desires. There are times that we, as parents, might beat ourselves up for not being able to give what we think we need to give to our children. Then there are times when our children teach us lessons about life. These lessons can be so profound and life-changing, or they could even be as subtle as a brief statement from a twelve-year-old. "I thought this place was an all-you-can-eat place"!

Take time to learn from your children. We can learn from them if we listen and are open to hearing what they tell us.

First Born

My little children, let us not love in word or in tongue, but in deed and truth. 1 John 3:18

There are many "firsts" that we encounter when we are a young couple. We get to experience our first apartment together, our first purchase of a home together, our first trip together, our first illness together, our first pregnancy together, and yes, our first birth together. Let's picture a young couple, high school sweethearts who get married at ages twenty and eighteen. The husband is in the Army, leaves his first duty station in Korea, comes home to marry his sweetheart, and the couple moves off immediately after the wedding to Fort Hood, Texas. This was my story in 1984.

While at Fort Hood, my first wife, Shirley, and I learned of our pregnancy, and excitement arrived with the news. Excitement mixed with anxiety, fear, and anticipation struck me as we confirmed what we believed to be true; we were expecting our firstborn. I remember vividly, one morning, staring out the dining area window in our rented house in Temple, Texas, tearing up with a combination of excitement and fear. I remember Shirley asking me what was wrong. I told her how fearful I was of making mistakes in raising our child. She lovingly reassured me that I would be a good dad and not to compare myself to my upbringing. You see, my dad was a dad that commanded respect, ruled with an iron fist, loved his family, and worked tirelessly to provide for and support his family. As I reflect on that, I was fearful of ruling with an iron fist type of mentality. Thankfully, God matched me up with a wife who was to become a terrific mother to all five of our children, and as we both learned, the parenting process began.

A short fifteen months at Fort Hood, Texas, led me to my next duty station in Darmstadt, Germany. Shirley was pregnant with our first son, David, and I left to go overseas. As I began my tour in Germany, my primary focus was to get military housing so that Shirley could fly there before her "no-fly" date and we could be together for the upcoming birth. Fortunately, shortly after I got there, I could move into housing. Shirley was able to fly to Germany eight months pregnant, and we were able to move into our military apartment three to four weeks before David arrived.

So, here we are, very young, in our second year of marriage, living overseas in a foreign country, with no vehicle, not a whole bunch of friends, and getting to experience all this together. Talk about a learning experience! We learned how to lean on each other and friends when we needed it. As I recall, Shirley entered labor late in the evening on the 6th of December 1985! I was freaking out. You see, now that it's "go time," I didn't have the means to go! We had no car! So now, what was I to do? Many details are foggy, but I remember walking from our apartment complex, about a half mile off base, to our unit. Yes, I had to leave Shirley by herself until I got back.

Once at my unit, I was able to get some help. I checked in with the duty NCO; we contacted my supervisor, who was very helpful and guided me in how we were to get Shirley and me to the hospital, which was not, by the way, in Darmstadt, where I was stationed. The military hospital was in Frankfurt, which was about a forty-five-minute drive. MSG Whitesides allowed the duty driver that night to drive Shirley and me to the hospital, so off we went. Mark and I jump in the military passenger vehicle, pick Shirley up at the apartment, and then drive to the hospital in Frankfurt while freaking out!

So, this is the story of how our firstborn son came into this world. Early December in Germany is very cold. That walk to my unit was cold and dark, but my adrenaline flowed. If memory serves me correctly, I had only a blue jean jacket, blue jeans, and a ball cap, a true South Louisiana boy in an unfamiliar environment. But we made it to the hospital, thanks to the expert driving of Mark, one of the few friends we had made since we arrived in the country, got checked in, and then I found out, for the very first time, how labor goes and how delivering a baby happens.

I had no clue! None. Totally in the dark, and all this was new. Did you know mothers in military hospitals were not given epidurals in the early eighties? Yeah, Shirley gave birth "naturally." I can remember her having back pain, which I learned was something called back labor, and how the only relief she could get was by me applying pressure and massaging her lower back. I also learned that you don't just check in to the hospital; tell them your wife is having a baby, and you get to hold and see your new addition to the family in a couple of hours. This process is a process! Hmm, who knew, right? Surely not me. Many lessons were learned that night. Childbirth is not something to be fearful of; it is something to be excited about and celebrate with each other. Birthing a child takes a long time, and no two births are identical. One of the main things for me to do during labor was not to ask too many questions, ask the right questions, tell my wife I love her, but not too often, don't attempt to comfort her during a contraction, and never hold her hand during a contraction! This last one is a selfish measure to save the possible bone-crushing in your hand. I learned that night that a woman suddenly gains superhuman strength when she goes into labor. I believe God designed it that way, and she must have the strength to go through the process, especially with no medication! So, remember, guys, hold her hand, but when that contraction starts coming, let it go!

After twelve grueling hours of ice chips, back spasms, and one contraction after another, it was time we met our first-born son, Clay "David" Morris Jr. He was born a very big boy, although not as big as others, but on the larger side of babies at nine pounds and fourteen ounces, and twenty-three and three-quarter inches long. Oh, and did I mention eighteen days overdue! I will tell you this: The experience of being there during childbirth with your wife is unlike anything ever. Witnessing the miracle of life is an incredible thing. I shed tears of joy whenever I saw David for the first time and did so for each of our five children. The emotion of seeing your child take their first breath is just unbelievable. Shirley and I were blessed to have gone through this together, thousands of miles from our families, and learned what it was like to lean on each other. So, our parenting process began that day, on December 7, 1985, and hasn't stopped.

Parenting 101 was now in session! Many lessons were learned along the way. Many failures, many successes, many happy times, many sorrowful times. Many laughs, many tears. Many lives were impacted, and many more to come! As you have read this, I hope you have been able to reflect on your life and your experience with childbirth. Whether you are the one doing all the work, mom, or you're the one in the support role, the blessing is going through it together. I pray for success over you; however, you define successful parenting. If I could offer one suggestion or recommendation, I would tell you to enjoy and cherish the process. Happy memories, my friends!

Hang in There, Son!

For He shall give His angels chare over you, To keep you in all your ways. Psalms 91:11

All four of my sons were student-athletes. I spent countless hours at baseball diamonds, basketball gyms, and football fields. When they were younger, I spent time assisting whoever was the head coach and doing what I could to help the boys. I watched them play through pain and rain in the damp, bone-chilling South Louisiana cold and the extreme summer heat of Northwest Florida. I have watched them grow as young men and watched the life lessons learned in the field of play be used as young adults. I have seen them grow as leaders, team players, and as family men of character and strength. I have also seen them in pain, emotional pain as well as physical pain.

Once, such an event happened while my third son, Gregg, was in high school. As usual, I was working the chains on the sideline. I had done so for almost every home game since his brothers began playing and continued to do so for sixteen years. It was my way of being close to the action and avoiding negative comments in the stands, but that's a subject for another story.

Gregg was always a very skilled football player that was blessed with much natural ability and developed grit and determination to work hard and give it everything he could. I remember early in the game; he was on the field as part of the kickoff team, and he sprinted down the field and put himself in a position to help his teammates make the tackle. It was a very normal play, not a super vicious hit; nothing spectacular happened, just a normal play. As I was standing on the visitor sideline holding the down marker, my vision followed Gregg off the field of play, where I noticed he went down to a knee right after he came off the field. His teammates and trainer were around him and helped him to the trainer's table, where I lost sight of him. This is where things get a little crazy.

I got a text message from my oldest son telling me something was wrong with Gregg. I immediately leave the down marker with another dad and hustle over to the sideline, where I see my son shivering. It was early fall in Louisiana and not cold at all. He was very pale, and the look in his eyes was filled with fear. Coach Hutson, the athletic trainer for the high school, looks at me and says we will send him to the hospital by ambulance. I hugged him big, said, "Hang in there, son," and went to the hospital.

My youngest son, Ryan, whom I will introduce to you in another story, was a freshman at the time and still playing. As I remember, my oldest son, David, was at the game, and he stayed with Ryan until afterward, and his mother and I met up at the hospital.

Gregg was immediately taken back for evaluation upon arrival at the emergency room, another sign that this was very serious. Even though I was not walking as a Christian then, I prayed for my son. I prayed for his doctors; I prayed for I don't know what. All I know is that I prayed. After an eternity, we finally received word that Gregg had an enlarged spleen. This came about as a result of having mononucleosis, which we didn't know he had either! His only symptoms for this were some tiredness, so nobody had any idea he had been ill. Someone hit him in the back on that tackle because of the team's philosophy of gang tackling and meeting at the ball. Well, this contact was enough to cause a problem with his spleen. The doctor and nurses on staff were incredible, and Gregg became a fan favorite while there. Gregg remained hospitalized until all was healed and he became very inspired by his nurse, a young man who spoke life into Gregg and initially motivated Gregg to pursue nursing. Gregg's career path changed as God eventually revealed His calling upon Gregg's life as a coach and teacher of our young people.

I can remember Gregg only being worried about how the game was going. He's always been such a competitor, and true to form, this situation was no different. I kept getting updates from the game and passing them along to him. Honestly, I don't even remember if they won, but I am certain that Gregg could tell you, and he could also tell you the final score. He was just so into his teammates and team; he wanted them to succeed. I would say that any athlete wants to see their teammates be successful, but this situation opened my eyes to a son that even though the look in his eyes-only hours before had been a look of extreme fear, he wanted only the best for his team.

Gregg carried this team first and team player mentality with him everywhere. He brought it to the basketball court, where he was often the sixth or seventh man. He brought it to the baseball field. He brought it to college, where he truly played as a team player when asked; or told to change positions from wide receiver to tight end, thus reducing his playing time but utilizing his skills as a downfield blocker to best help his team.

God spared my son that day. He has allowed Gregg to play football at the collegiate level, just as all of his brothers did, to get a college degree, and today he is a high school football coach on the field where this incident/injury occurred and a girls' basketball coach in the very gym he grew up being that team player. God has given Gregg the grit and determination to win in life and sports. He has gifted Gregg with the desire and passion for leading young men and women to be the best they can be, inspiring and motivating them, and helping them achieve their dreams. He has placed in Gregg a caring heart and love for his family that is making him an incredible husband to his wife and high school sweetheart, Katelyn, and his super special son, Julien (JuJu); as well as at the time of this writing, Gregg and Katelyn's second child to be joining our family this year.

God has a plan for Gregg, and that's why we didn't lose our son that night back in 2009! God is not done with him yet, and Gregg is not done impacting lives! His Word tells us in the familiar verse from Jeremiah 29:11, "For I know the thoughts that I think toward you, says the Lord, thoughts of peace and not of evil, to give you a future and a hope."

Gregg, you matter. You are making a difference, and to all whom God allows to read this, you matter also, and you are making a difference as well. As you read this story from our life, I pray that you are inspired to reflect on yours and see God's blessings and equipment in your life. Allow God to use you to impact your impact zones!

Bonus Kids

My little children, let us not love in word or in tongue, but in deed and in truth. 1 John 3:18

When two people marry, the couple is marrying each other, but they are also marrying each other's families. I believe this is especially true when there are children involved. When Michelle and I first married, this was a lesson I had to learn, and I must admit, this road was a little bumpy. It was a lot bumpy. Okay, so let's be honest; this road was filled with potholes, poor signage, and no guardrails. It was a road I had never been down before, but one I was willing to try and navigate. Part of the family dynamics in our relationship was the blending of families. I had moved in with Michelle and her two teenage children and, thus, began the learning process.

My bonus family consisted of many nights in the early parts of our relationship where I had to learn. I had to learn how to deal with a teenage girl whose emotions were worn on her sleeve, and she could cry at the drop of a hat. Even though I had a daughter of my own, Abby was nowhere near her teenage years, so this was a new experience for me. Jackie, my bonus daughter, taught me numerous things. She, along with her mom, taught Sergeant Morris to dial back the tone of his voice and speak softer and more caring. I had no idea that I was as gruff as I was, but looking back at it, I can certainly see the hard shell of my military service and how I allowed it to be what defined me. This is not a bad thing, but when you are dealing with the emotions of a teenage girl, it quickly becomes apparent that I must learn a new language.

I remember vividly; I was at home one day when Jackie came into the bedroom crying hysterically. Her sobs were scary, and yes, it freaked me out. I tried to talk to her and was making zero progress. Finally, I called her mom and said, "Jackie is freaking out; she's crying uncontrollably and will not stop. I have no idea why and can't understand what she's trying to tell me through the emotional outburst! What do I do?" Michelle calmly told me to hold her. Just be there for her, hold her, and let her cry. So, I did. I sat on the bathroom floor, told Jackie to sit with me, and held her while she cried it out. We sat there for a good twenty to thirty minutes until she was through the crisis and then got up, and everything was okay. If you were to ask me what her meltdown was about, to this day, neither one of us could remember. But we do remember the lessons we both learned about each other. I learned that sometimes no words need to be spoken, and it's okay just to hold on and cry. Jackie learned that I could be there, that she could depend on me to be there in body and spirit. Jackie and I continue to grow our relationship and lean on each other. We continue to grow and constantly teach each other new things, and I am so grateful for my bonus daughter.

Now, let's talk a little bit about bonus sons. Wade is Michelle's oldest child and was eighteen when we got together. I had mentored him in a military boot camp-style youth challenge program, in which he seemed to excel, and he even got his GED equivalent diploma during this training. When I moved in, though, I met a young man who seemed to want to exert his dominance as the alpha male in the home. We clashed from the beginning. This was extremely tough for me to wrap my head around since I had four boys of my own and had been able to, along with the help of their mother, instill a sense of commitment, pride, determination, integrity, and servanthood to name a few character traits in our boys. Wade, however, was not down with that at all.

He and I were in each other's faces numerous times, trying to force our dominance on each other. Neither of us would back down, and neither of us would let the other know we were faltering. These encounters continued until we both realized we didn't have to live at odds with each other. I can remember one time when I removed the door to his room. I was not happy with how he was cleaning, or not cleaning, his room, and I just removed the door off the hinges and moved it. We didn't speak for days. We were so ticked off at each other. I eventually learned that this type of communication and discipline only worsens matters. It's like trying to toss a little extra gasoline into a fire that is already going. What will happen is that the fire will follow the fuel back to the container of fuel and blow up. This is what door removals and such will do. It will cause things to escalate and do so quickly!

Wade and I both had to grow; this was not a short process. This process has taken us at least ten to eleven years. We both have learned that neither one of us will leave Michelle, and we are better with each other in our lives. Wade has taught me patience. He has taught me to reach out for mentoring and help. He has taught me that it's okay to see things differently than I do. He has taught me that we are all unique creations of God, the God of the universe, the God that loves us enough to allow us to grow, and the God of forgiveness.

Wade and I learned that we needed to forgive each other and ourselves. We both still have strong personalities, but we understand that we can depend on each other when needed. Over the years, I have been there for Wade, and he has been there for me. We have grown together, matured, and accepted each other as important parts of our wonderful, blended family. Thanks, Wade, for your instruction, and I know you will continue to improve just as I am.

Bonus and blended families can be very interesting. They can be very challenging. They can be very rewarding as well. I am thankful that we have a blended family that continues to get closer to each other we all grow and learn more about our history, our vision for our future, and our love. It takes action to increase one's belief. That action is exemplified in our word and deed, just as it says in the Bible. If you have a blended family, I encourage you never to give up and act, not just speak words. We must show our family how much we love them, so let's go out today and be intentional about our actions and show our children, and bonus children, that we love them!

A Champion's Heart

And whatever you do, do it heartily, as to the Lord and not to men, knowing that from the Lord you will receive the reward of the inheritance: for you serve the Lord Christ. Colossians 3:23-24

The following is a quote from November 11, 2017. It is from my youngest son, Ryan, who was preparing for the final time he would ever suit up and play the game of football. He states,

Game Day! The last game day I will ever experience as a player. It is bittersweet. These are pictures from my first year of football and ETBU a few weeks ago. I love the last one because it shows exactly how I have played this game for the past twelve years. Every fourth quarter I put my fists up to show that I am going to fight to the very end. That is exactly what I intend to do today. I have told my teammates I can't promise we will be victorious, but I can promise that I won't quit fighting until the last second rolls off the clock. In all things, I want people to know why I play this game the way I do. I am using every bit of athletic potential God has blessed me with to glorify him. I am not playing for myself or even win (although it's nice to win, and you should never strive to lose). I am playing for something much bigger: To glorify the one true God. I pray that those who have seen me play and played with me can see that.

Ryan has always been a tough dude. I remember how determined he was to be with his older brothers and do the things they did when he was very young. The nickname Ryno became indicative of the mental toughness this kid had. You see, Ryno has always been the hardest working, most dedicated, and passionate young man on any ball field, basketball court, or ministry arena that was out there. From a very young age, his work ethic set him above most. I want to say that I contributed to that; however, thirteen years ago, at the time of this writing, I made a decision that greatly affected his youth. I decided to step out of my twenty-five-year marriage. This decision impacted Ryan greatly. To be blunt and transparent, it made him very angry. He truly hated me for this. This story, though, is about Ryan and the heart of a champion. Know that it took many years of reconciliatory efforts to gain the closeness we have today. Many tears have been shed, many prayers have been spoken, and many conversations have had to be held to move to where we are today. I am grateful to be where I am and extremely thankful for forgiveness and grace.

Ryno's heart was hardened back then, and his determination was channeled on the gridiron, where he played with a purpose. Ryan played only one position in twelve years of football, and that position was center. He had always been a leader and led by example. From the first time he played, it was a position that seemed natural for him, even though his stature was small. In college, he was blessed with only a height of 5'10" and hands that were small as compared to most offensive linemen. He made up for what he lacked in physical size in his heart. In his famous Just Do It speech, Art Williams once said, "There ain't nobody ever designed a test, nor will they design a test, that can measure the heart of a man or woman."[5] If I didn't know any better, I would think Art was speaking directly about Ryan. His heart led his teams into battle every week on game day. Without fail, he sprinted from the sideline to the center of the field every time his offense went back onto the field. After every play, he would run from the huddle to the line of scrimmage. He did this not to bring eyes to himself but to be an example of grit. His mental toughness, as he played this game, was unquestioned. He set the example for hustle and grit. See, Ryan was a warrior, a leader, and an example-setter. He had a burning desire to be the absolute best version of himself he could be every day. Ryno was not playing this game for himself. He wasn't playing this game for his brothers. He wasn't playing this game for his coaches. He was playing this game for God, for the one true God, the God of the universe, the God who created everything, the God who carried him when he needed carrying.

The words Ryan shared that day in 2017 were from his heart. They were from the heart of a champion. They were from the heart of someone with a pure servant's heart and a character's heart. I pray that Ryan's words will inspire all who read them. Ryan received his undergraduate degree in 2018, moved on to Medical School, and graduated in May of 2021 as Doctor Ryan Morris. Ryno never quit. He overcame many obstacles in the field of play, in the classroom, and at home. The never quit mentality he has always shown is an example to even his father. I look at this young man with respect, admiration, and, most of all, gratitude; gratitude is a result of the grace he has shown me and the grace that our God has shown me as we continue life's journey.

I share this part of Ryan's story to encourage you to be an overcomer. Be a person of great character that serves something and someone greater than yourself. Be that person with the grit and determination to never give up on yourself or your team. Be that person that is part of something so much greater than yourself. Let Ryan's story become your story. Let Ryan's example become your example, and never give up! You are a winner. You are a champion, and you have a heart of a champion, just like Ryan! Embrace your path, and work heartily for the Lord rather than men (see Col. 3:23).

Crispy Parma Pork & Pasta

Ingredients

PORK:

- 8 center-cut loin chops
- 3 tbsp. garlic roasted olive oil
- 8 oz. Parmesan, freshly grated
- 1/3 cup seasoned breadcrumbs
- 1/4 cup fresh parsley, chopped
- 3 tsp. garlic and pepper seasoning
- 1 tsp. smoked paprika
- 1 tsp. Kosher salt

- 1 stick of unsalted butter, cut into 1 tbsp. slices
- 3 additional tbsps. roasted garlic olive oil
- 3 eggs
- 1/2 tbsp. hot sauce
- PASTA:
- 2 lbs. extra wide egg noodles
- 1 tsp. olive oil
- 1 tsp. Kosher salt
- 1/4 cup Parmesan, freshly grated
- 1 tbsp. garlic and pepper seasoning

GARNISH:
- fresh paprika, finely chopped
- Parmesan cheese, freshly grated

Directions

1. Cut center-cut pork loin into one-inch-thick chops.
2. Sprinkle garlic roasted olive oil onto chops and lightly rub on both sides.
3. Preheat oven to 425 degrees.
4. Spray two 9 x 13 baking dishes thoroughly with cooking spray and set them to the side.
5. In a medium size mixing bowl, combine the following ingredients well: grated Parmesan, breadcrumbs, fresh parsley, garlic and pepper seasoning, smoked paprika, and Kosher salt.
6. In a second smaller mixing bowl, combine the eggs and hot

sauce. Use a fork or small wire whisk to beat the eggs and mix well.
7. Place a skillet on the stove (I prefer cast iron.) at medium-high heat. Add three pats of butter.
8. Once the skillet is hot, and the butter is melted, dip the pork chop into the egg mixture, then dredge through the breadcrumb mixture, ensuring the chop is completely covered on both sides.
9. Gently place in skillet and sear for three to four minutes on each side.
10. Remove from skillet and place in pre-greased baking dish and repeat until all chops are seared.
11. Place remaining pats of butter in baking dishes with pork chops.
12. Place baking dishes in the oven for twenty minutes or until the internal temperature is 145 degrees.
13. In a large pot, pour four to five cups of water for pasta, adding a pinch of salt and a few sprinkles of olive oil.
14. Bring water to a boil, add pasta, and return to boil.
15. Reduce heat, cover, and let simmer until pasta is tender.
16. Strain pasta, add one tablespoon of garlic and pepper seasoning, and one-quarter cup of freshly grated Parmesan.
17. Remove pork chops from the oven.
18. Place pasta onto the plate.
19. Place pork chop on top of pasta.
20. Sprinkle garnish over top of pork and pasta.

Note:

Be certain to cook pork to an internal temperature of at least 145 degrees.

Garlic-Parmesan Chicken Wings

Ingredients

- ➢ 3 dozen chicken wings
- ➢ 2 tsp. Kosher salt
- ➢ 1 tbsp. garlic powder
- ➢ 2 tbsp. garlic and pepper seasoning
- ➢ 1/3 cup fresh parsley, coarsely chopped
- ➢ 1/4 cup garlic, minced
- ➢ 1 stick of unsalted butter
- ➢ 1/4 cup of garlic butter with Parmesan and basil (from your local grocer)

Directions

1. Clean and prep chicken wings by rinsing in cool water, removing the wing tip, and cutting the joint between the drumette and the flat.

Note: A good pair of kitchen shears or sharp chef's knives will come in handy here.

2. Lightly spray a baking pan with cooking spray and preheat the oven to 400 degrees.
3. Place chicken wings onto your baking pan and gently dry both sides with a paper towel.
4. In a small mixing bowl, place your Kosher salt, garlic salt, and garlic and pepper seasoning and stir to mix well.
5. Generously sprinkle seasoning mixture over dried chicken wings and place in your 400-degree oven for approx. Forty-five minutes.

Note: Use the center rack of your oven to ensure the bottom half doesn't scorch or vice-versa.

6. While baking, pour finely grated fresh Parmesan, coarsely chopped fresh parsley, and minced garlic into a large mixing bowl with a lid.
7. Place the unsalted and garlic-seasoned butter in a separate saucepan and set aside.
8. When the chicken is done (golden brown on top), remove it from the oven to rest while you melt the butter.

9. Melt the two kinds of butter, add to your mixing bowl of Parmesan cheese mixture, and stir well.
10. Now the magic! Remove the chicken wings from the pan and place them into the mixing bowl with your garlic, butter, and Parmesan.
11. Place the lid on the bowl and shake the bowl to mix the chicken with the garlic seasoning thoroughly.
12. Use a pair of tongs to remove the chicken from the bowl and plate it.

Option: Take just a little fresh parsley and lightly sprinkle it over the wings.

Parmesan Shrimp Avocado Garlic Bread

Ingredients

- 1 loaf of New Orleans French bread
- 1/4 cup unsalted butter, melted
- 1/2 tsp. garlic powder
- 1 tsp. garlic, finely minced
- 1 tsp. Italian paprika
- 1 tbsp. garlic-infused avocado oil
- 1 lb. shrimp, peeled and deveined
- 1/4 cup fresh parsley, finely chopped
- 1 avocado cut up into bite-sized portions

- 1 cup cherry tomatoes, cut in half
- 1-1/2 tbsp. lemon juice
- salt and pepper to taste
- 1/4 cup Parmesan cheese, freshly grated

Directions

1. Place shrimp, garlic, paprika, and lemon juice in a mixing bowl and mix well by hand, ensuring the shrimp get a good coating of all ingredients.
2. Place a cast-iron skillet on a med-high temp on the stove and pour one tablespoon of garlic-infused avocado oil into the skillet.
3. Once the pan is hot, add the shrimp mixture and cook on each side for two to three minutes. Be careful you do not overcook the shrimp. They should turn a light pinkish color.
4. Remove from heat, sprinkle with the fresh parsley, and set aside.
5. Preheat the oven to a low broil setting.
6. Mix well with your avocado, tomatoes, lemon juice, and salt and pepper in a large bowl.
7. Add the shrimp mixture and gently stir to mix so the avocado does not fall apart , and set aside.
8. Prepare your baking sheet by lightly spraying it with a non-stick cooking spray.
9. Cut French bread in half and place both halves on the baking sheet
10. Combine your melted unsalted butter, garlic powder, and minced garlic in a bowl and spread evenly onto the French bread.

11. Place bread in the oven for a few minutes and remove when it is turned a light golden brown on top.
12. Remove the bread from the oven and cut it into smaller pieces.
13. Scoop the shrimp and avocado mixture onto the pieces of garlic bread.
14. Place onto a serving place, lightly sprinkle with grated Parmesan cheese and serve.

Note:

Shrimp should be cooked to an internal temp of 145 degrees Fahrenheit.

Tip to tell when done:

While cooking shrimp in a skillet or grill, pay close attention to the crevice in the back of the shrimp where the vein was removed, which will be opposite the tail end and the thickest part of the shrimp. Once the shrimp turns opaque, it is done.

Roasted Pork with Garlic Parmesan Cream Sauce

Ingredients

- ➤ 3-4 lb. boneless pork loin
- ➤ 1/2 cup butter, garlic, and jalapeno marinade
- ➤ 2 tbsp. garlic and pepper seasoning
- ➤ 3 tbsp. roasted garlic olive oil
- ➤ 1/2 cup beef broth
- ➤ 6 cloves of fresh garlic, minced
- ➤ 1/2 cup all-purpose flour
- ➤ 2 cups (plus/minus) half-n-half

- 4 tbsp. Parmesan cheese, freshly grated
- 2 tbsp. fresh parsley, chopped
- 1 lb. linguine pasta
- 2 pinches of Kosher salt
- 1 tsp. olive oil

Directions

1. Take half of a pork loin, and inject thoroughly with a garlic-infused injection. (I used butter, garlic, and jalapeno injection)
2. Sprinkle garlic and ground pepper seasoning onto both sides of the pork.
3. Pour the remaining injection over the pork, cover it, and place it in the refrigerator for at least one hour. (I always try to let them marinate for six to eight hours.)
4. When ready to cook, remove the pork from the refrigerator, preheat the oven to 350 degrees, and spray the roasting pan/pot with non-stick cooking spray.
5. Place pan on a stovetop burner over med-med/high heat.
6. Add roasted garlic olive oil to the pan.
7. Remove the pork loin from the marinade pan and place it into the roasting pan on the stovetop: **Do not discard excess marinade/injection.**
8. Sear both sides, top and bottom of pork loin.
9. Pour the remaining marinade/injection over top of the seared pork loin.
10. Add half a cup of beef broth.

11. Cover and place in preheated oven.
12. While pork is roasting in the oven, you will want to cook your linguine. Add two pinches of Kosher salt and one tablespoon of olive oil while cooking your pasta, strain it, and have it ready as soon as the sauce is finished.
13. After forty-five minutes, check the pork loin temp; it should be between 145 degrees and 150 degrees. Be careful not to overcook; temperatures higher than this can cause pork to dry out.
14. Remove from the oven, set on the stovetop, leave covered, and let rest for fifteen minutes.
15. Carefully remove the pork loin from the pan and place it on a large cutting board.
16. Slice pork loin into three-quarter to one-inch slices, place it on a separate pan, cover it, so it does not dry out, and set aside.
17. Place the roasting pan used to roast the pork loin on the stovetop and heat the juices back up. Using a wooden spatula, scrape the good drippings off the bottom of the roaster! Add the minced garlic to the juices and sauté for about three minutes.
18. Add shavings and pieces off the cutting board from slicing the pork.
19. Slowly add flour while stirring constantly. This will thicken up the rue. Be careful not to allow it to stick to the bottom of the roaster, as we don't want to lose all the goodness from the drippings.
20. Slowly add half and half while stirring constantly. This will

lighten the color and thin out our cream sauce. Continue to add and stir until you achieve desired consistency. Remember, this is a sauce and not gravy. This sauce should be fairly thick but thin enough to pour over our pasta and pork easily.

21. Add four tablespoons of freshly grated Parmesan and two tablespoons of fresh chopped parsley to your sauce and stir thoroughly.
22. Create a linguine bed on your plate, place sliced pork onto the linguine, and pour cream sauce over your pork and pasta.
23. Sprinkle two to three pinches of grated Parmesan over the serving.
24. Garnish with one to two pinches of loosely chopped fresh parsley and serve.

Note: This sauce will thicken rather quickly as it sits. Should this happen, just pour a little more half-and-half over low heat, and stir until it loosens back up.

Sunshine Shrimp Pasta

Ingredients

- ➤ 1 lb. linguine pasta
- ➤ 1 lb. shrimp, peeled and deveined
- ➤ 1 lb. smoked sausage
- ➤ 1 tbsp. garlic pepper
- ➤ 1 tbsp. smoked paprika
- ➤ 1 tbsp. smoked bacon salt
- ➤ 1 large pinch of Kosher salt
- ➤ 2 tbsp. minced garlic
- ➤ 3 tbsp. unsalted butter

- 1 tsp. roasted garlic olive oil
- Juice from 1/2 lemon
- Juice from 1/2 lime
- 1-1/2 tbsp. Creole seasoning

Directions

1. Peel and devein shrimp and place in a medium size bowl.
2. Add dry ingredients: garlic pepper, smoked paprika, smoked bacon salt, Kosher salt, and Creole seasoning to shrimp, blend well by hand, and set to the side. Be sure to place them in the refrigerator if it takes longer than about thirty minutes to prep the remaining items.
3. Slice one pound of your favorite smoked sausage into small discs then cut those in half.
4. Place three tablespoons of unsalted butter in a deep skillet and set the heat to medium.
5. Place about four cups of water, a splash of olive oil, and a dash of salt in a pot large enough to boil one pound of linguine and turn the heat to high and bring water to a boil.
6. Add linguine noodles to boiling water, stir well, bring back to a boil, lower heat to medium/low and allow the pasta to cook for about twelve to fifteen minutes.
7. Place smoked sausage into preheated and buttered skillet and brown sausage.
8. Once the sausage is browned to your desired char, place pre-seasoned shrimp into a skillet with sausage and cook until the

shrimp are a light pink color.
9. Lightly squeeze juice from half of a lemon and half of a lime into the skillet; be sure not to drop any seeds from the fruit into the skillet.
10. Remove cooked pasta from the stove, strain pasta, and add pasta to the deep skillet with shrimp and sausage.
11. Stir pasta to mix with all the meat thoroughly.
12. Add more Creole seasoning, salt, or black pepper if you like.
13. Serve it up, and enjoy!

Special Diet Information

This recipe does contain shellfish; if you are allergic to any shellfish, please do not consume it.

Bacon Wrapped Buffalo Chicken

Ingredients

- 2 lbs. boneless skinless chicken thighs
- 1 lb. thick-cut bacon
- 3 tbsp. buffalo rub
- 1/2 cup buffalo sauce
- 1 tbsp. olive oil

Directions

1. Cut boneless skinless chicken thighs in half or thirds (bite-sized pieces).

2. Place in a large mixing bowl.
3. Cut the slab of bacon in half and set it aside.
4. Sprinkle buffalo rub over chicken.
5. Pour buffalo sauce onto the chicken.
6. Combine well, ensuring sauce and rub are evenly distributed over chicken pieces.
7. Preheat the convection oven or conventional oven to 350.
8. Pour olive oil into the skillet, ensuring you coat the entire bottom.
9. Wrap each piece of chicken with a piece of bacon.
10. Place bacon-wrapped chicken into the skillet, leaving a little room between each piece.
11. Place skillet into the preheated oven for approximately twenty-five to thirty minutes or until bacon is crispy.
12. Remove from oven.
13. Using a set of tongs or a spatula, remove the chicken from the skillet and place it on a serving plate.

Note: I recommend you serve it immediately while hot, along with your favorite dipping sauce.

Baked Stuffed Chicken Breast

Ingredients

- 5 large chicken breasts
- 5 links mild sweet Italian sausage
- 1 block of cream cheese
- 2 pinches of Kosher salt
- smokey garlic and onion seasoning
- drizzle of hot sauce (optional)
- 5 pats of butter

Directions

1. Cut the breast open by butterflying them the entire length of the breast without cutting all the way through.
2. Open the flap and lightly season with the smokey garlic and onion seasoning.
3. Slice the block of cream cheese lengthwise into five equal slices.
4. Place the slice of cream cheese in the fold of the breast.
5. Remove the skin from the Italian sausage links and place the ground sausage in the fold on top of the cream cheese.
6. Fold the flap over and pat down to flatten the stuffing.
7. Generously sprinkle both sides of the folded breast with smokey garlic and onion seasoning.
8. Splash a few drops of hot sauce on each chicken breast (optional).
9. Sprinkle Kosher salt over the breasts.
10. Preheat oven to 350.
11. Place breasts in a lightly greased Dutch oven or skillet and place one pat of butter on each breast.
12. Once the oven gets to temp, place an uncovered Dutch oven or skillet in the oven on the top rack for one hour.
13. Remove and set for three to five minutes, plate, and serve with your favorite side dish.

Italian Chicken Pasta

Ingredients

- 3 boneless skinless chicken breasts cut into 1/2" thick strips
- roasted garlic avocado oil
- 1-1/2 tsp. Kosher salt
- 1 tsp. garlic powder
- 1 tsp. onion powder
- 1 tsp. garlic pepper seasoning
- 1 tsp. Italian seasoning
- 1/4 cup chicken marinade
- 1 tsp. minced garlic

- ➢ 1 lb. cooked pasta
- ➢ 1-1/2 cups of marinara sauce

Directions

1. On medium-high heat, place chicken in a preheated skillet with one-fourth of a cup of avocado oil.
2. Pan-sear chicken thoroughly, ensuring the chicken is completely done.
3. Heat marinara sauce. (I use a product made and sold locally.)
4. Add seasonings to taste.
5. Place cooked pasta on a plate.
6. Ladle a small bit of marinara on a bed of pasta.
7. Place two chicken strips on marinara-covered pasta.
8. Lightly spoon a little more marinara over the top of the chicken strips.
9. Sprinkle with grated Parmesan cheese, mozzarella, or both

Christmas Traditions

For unto us a Child is born, Unto us a Son is given; And the government will be upon His shoulder. And His name will be called Wonderful, Counselor, Mighty God, Everlasting Father, Prince of Peace. Isaiah 9:6

Christmas! Ah, what a wonderful time of year! Many memories are created around this joyous time of year. Families often reconnect around the baked ham, sweet potatoes, and green bean casserole, or in the case of many of us in South Louisiana, we gather around a big ole pot of seafood or chicken & sausage gumbo! Yes, Christmas is a very special time of year. A time when traditions are continued and, yes, even begun. It is a time when many of us use this time to slow our lives down just a bit and enjoy time with family and friends. Many of us have traditions we share with those same people, the ones in our inner circle, the ones that mean the most to us, the ones we hope will one day keep some of our traditions going.

As we reflect on Christmas, we might recognize that many things we do and how we do them are passed on to us from others. Their traditions can easily become our traditions if we choose. Let's look at some of my Christmas traditions as I hope to inspire you to reflect on some of your very own. Maybe you used to follow some traditions but stopped, which might encourage you to start back up. You see, friends, there's no right or wrong way to have a tradition. You can start one now, provided you do it consistently and pass it down to your children, thus calling it a tradition.[6]

As a very young child, one of my earliest memories of a tradition was the gathering of all of my mom's side of the family at her parent's house. Maw Maw would spend hours and hours cooking. She would make mirliton casserole, homemade lemon meringue pies, and banana pudding, and yes, as always, she had those amazing biscuits. I thankfully was able to recreate and share that recipe in my first book *Inspired Cooking*. Everyone brought a little food and PRESENTS! As a child, my highlight was seeing what everyone brought ME! It was all about me, and that's okay because what I took from that was that as I got older, it transitioned to a giving mindset. I remember, we would open those presents after dinner, take our new favorite toys and play with our cousins for what seemed like hours; not in a bad way, but this was hours and hours of great times! I loved hanging out with my cousins, and even as we have grown much older and have our own families, it is always a wonderful time when I can meet up with any of them and reconnect. I remember all the men gathering around the card table for a game of Booray. I would walk by and see the piles of nickels, dimes, and quarters in front of my dad and all my uncles, and I couldn't wait until I was able to play. Some of these traditions from my childhood carried on to my adult life, and some didn't. It's okay not to bring some traditions, but I would say that not bringing any of your childhood traditions with you as an adult would not only shortchange your children but would eventually stop your heritage from being passed on.

When two people get married, traditions are combined, and new traditions are formed. Many times, you might see a young family hold on to something from their childhood, and as they grow their family, they have the desire to create their traditions. This is exactly what happened when my first wife, Shirley, and I began our family. We brought traditions from each of our families and began to meld some of them with our own, and eventually, as our children have grown and begun their families, they have done the same. Some of the traditions we brought along with us was gathering around food. As I write this, I am easily reminded of how my passion for cooking and feeding people was breathed into me from an early age. Shirley's mom is a fantastic cook, and she has been gracious enough to share two of her recipes in this book. Mama G, as she is called by many, literally lived in the kitchen. She would come up with some of the most amazing things! I remember she would make these cookies called Hermits; they were simply delicious! I also remember her rum balls and whiskey balls which were tasty and spending time at Mama G's and Rabbit's, as Shirley's dad was called. I remember meeting together with her side of the family and playing games like Right-Left-Right, which was always led by our sister-in-law, Jamie. I remember playing football with all the boys while Shirley's brothers, Gordy, Bobby, and I, took turns playing quarterback. I remember spending time with her dad around the grill as he cooked the best porterhouse steaks I had tasted. These great times and times have also impacted my family and me. I remember the new traditions Shirley and I started. Traditions like watching the classic movie *It's a Wonderful Life*, where Jimmy Stewart plays George Bailey, and the story of how many lives one person can impact is told. Another tradition Shirley and I started was reading the Christmas story from the Bible just before we tucked all the kids in for bed. And yes, of course, one more tradition was for me to get up and cook a massive Christmas morning breakfast, often consisting of bacon, sausage, biscuits, gravy, eggs, or fried backstrap!

And still, when I married my second wife, Michelle, we blended our families, carried some traditions, and created some more! For example, we still watch *It's a Wonderful Life*, or at least some of it, as I usually fall asleep about halfway through. And yes, I still enjoy cooking a special Christmas breakfast. Probably the biggest tradition we have created is something our kids have named The Morris Family Extravaganza! This is a wonderfully joyous time where we all get together, all twenty-five to thirty of us, and enjoy each other! After we eat a terrific meal, we sit down and all the kids get to open their gifts, and it's just so exciting to see their faces light up. I can imagine that as I remember my childhood and our Christmases at Maw Maw's, my face was the same way, traditions!

There are so many ways we each celebrate the birth of our Jesus! I have shared a few memories from my past and hope I have inspired you to remember some of your own and even encouraged you to begin new ones that you might pass on to the next generation. Enjoy your memories. Cherish your memories. Cling to those memories and let them help you create your memories and traditions and make that generational impact!

High School Days – The Good Ole Days

being confident of this very thing, that He who has begun a good work in you will complete it until the day of Jesus Christ; Philippians 1:6

The good ole days. We often hear this phrase spoken and hear the reference back in the day or back when I was your age. Many of us might have even used these phrases or many others as we reminisce about our younger years. I think you would agree that our younger years, or more conveniently stated, the good ole days helped shape us into who we are and lay a foundation for our lives as an adult. These days may have been filled with fun, laughter, disappointment, and frustration. These days may have been difficult and trying as well as exciting and fun. I'm sure that as we think about the days we spent back in high school, we would all see many of these emotions that played a part in our growth and prepared us for life as grown folk.

I am currently partnered with a group of classmates from my senior class, and we are planning our fortieth high school graduation reunion. I find it exciting yet trying to reconnect with our classmates. We shared classrooms, gymnasiums, football fields, locker rooms, common areas, and events we participated in together. As we walked down the breezeway of Glen Oaks High School in Baton Rouge, Louisiana, we talked with our friends, laughed, and sometimes even fought with them. We would high-five a fellow football team member or band member as we passed each other and talked about our big plans for the weekend. We would look at that guy or girl that caught our eye and try to get the courage to ask them for a phone number or maybe if they'd go to a movie with us. We would run, laugh, sing, and dance. Our future was now, and life was good. We spent our days enjoying this time and just living for the moment, not thinking about tomorrow, the next day, two years down the road, ten years in our future, or even forty years! This was our time. When I think of the good ole days, these things come to mind as I think about our high school days.

Glen Oaks High School is a school nestled in North Baton Rouge, and when the class of eighty-two was there, our student body was culturally diverse for our day. We were about fifty-five to sixty percent African Americans, and the balance was Caucasian. I am forever grateful to have attended a diverse school such as this because I feel it played a major role in my successes in life. From my time in the military, where it was preached that there is only one color, and that color is green, to my current position at Nucor Steel, Louisiana, where we have an extremely diversified culture base, I have learned to respect other values and understand with a non-judging attitude other people's beliefs and core principles. I believe it has helped me cultivate cross-cultural friendships that have been long-lasting and equipped me with some of the tools needed for success in life. Life at G.O. was fun. It was fun because of the people. It was fun because of our interaction. It was fun because we made it fun.

I can remember many dances where we would get dressed up, get our dates and corsages, take pictures, go out to eat, and, yes, try our best to spice up our fun by trying to find a store that would sell us beer or wine so we could add to the cheerful event, often, we were unsuccessful in that trek, well until I turned eighteen in my senior year. You see, back in the day, here goes that saying again, the legal drinking age was eighteen, so when that happened, it was game on! I remember football games where we would load up on our school bus, which was painted in our school colors of black, white, and red, with our logo on it and my name tattooed rather painted on the side. I can also remember a rival school visiting us after they beat us on Friday night, painting our bus and several walls of our practice stadium and locker room. I remember how ticked off we were when we came in the next morning to grade the film. I remember the fight in our eyes and the determination to get even and make things right with our rivals. There were also other great times. Times like pep rallies, band concerts, school plays, choir concerts, and many other extra-curricular activities. I remember trips with the Key Club to conventions and training events, and I can also remember getting into trouble at some of them. I can also remember hanging out with our friends at their homes, with their parents, working on projects, watching TV, listening to music, and enjoying life. These were fun times, indeed. But they were not without trials and struggles. These good ole days were not just days of sunshine and rainbows.

There were also times of sadness—times we had to attend a classmate's funeral—times we cried on each other's shoulders and leaned on each other for strength. We sometimes relied on each other for success, help, and grace. There were times when we depended on each other to have our backs. And there were times when we were there for each other in losing our family members. I believe our true metal was formed in these darkest times of our school years. The foundation was laid for whom we became as adults and set the table for our futures. Each one of our graduating classes had its own set of circumstances. Circumstances range from low self-esteem to too much self-esteem. Circumstances range from alcohol or drug addiction to never even touching the stuff. Circumstances range from unplanned pregnancies to vows of chastity. Circumstances ranged from untimely deaths of classmates or family to trying to help and counsel those who were going through these events. Yes, life hits us and sometimes hits us quite hard and often, even as we grow up and live our best life in the good ole days. I can tell you one thing about our class of eighty-two, however, we were then, and remain now, a caring and resilient people!

As I reconnect with friends while I walk the campus of this great school, I am reminded of many wonderful things. I'm reminded of how we were always there for each other, no matter how large or small the situation was. I'm reminded of the never-quit mentality our athletic teams had. I'm reminded of the strong work ethic of our ROTC teams, band, pesters, pantherettes, flag and rifle team, and many others. I'm reminded of our faculty's leadership, who truly cared about us: Teachers like Mr. Warren, Mrs. Terrell, Ms. Trosclair, Mr. Jacob, Mrs. Buckles, Mrs. Singleton, Coach Worsham, Coach Bush, Coach Weatherspoon, and so many others. As I think about these good ole days, I'm reminded how important it is to be a part of a community. And I'm also reminded that a great foundation was laid for all my classmates and me.

I know without a shadow of a doubt that my God was watching over me then as He watches over me now. I know He protected many of my classmates and me from harm and gave us another chance at things when we didn't deserve it. I know He did this because His plan had not yet been completed. I know that my high school years, the good ole days, were a part of God's plan for my life and for each of us. Your good ole days are the same. They may have looked much different than mine, or they may have looked quite the same. But one thing is certain, God knew what He was doing, He knew what was coming then, and He knows what is coming now.

In Psalms 66:10, the psalmist writes, "For You, O God, have tested us; You have refined us as silver is refined." It is through scripture such as this that I am confident that God is in control yesterday, today, and tomorrow. I am just grateful he put me on the Glen Oaks High School campus back then and used that ground to lay the foundation for the man I am becoming.

I hope you have enjoyed our trip to North Baton Rouge and our visit with the class of 82! Maybe it has recalled some memories and relationships you had then that you might need to rekindle now. I would tell you not to wait or delay, as our days are numbered, and we truly do not know when our last day on this earth will be.

It's More than a Workplace

Finally, all of you be of one mind, having compassion for one another; love as brothers, be tenderhearted, be courteous; 1 Peter 3:8

There's one thing I have learned about workplaces. Sometimes, a workplace is more than just a place to collect a paycheck. I found this out firsthand in 2011 when I decided to join a team that would become more than a team.

In my first book, "Inspired Cooking," I introduced you to my best buddy, Tony, and you learned how we first met. Just know the story continued. After he retired from the Navy, Petty Officer Terry had to find another career. He landed in Memphis, Tennessee, thanks to a nudge from his brother-in-law, and was hired by a company that is much more than a company. As you are about to learn, Nucor Steel is much more than a workplace. After he began his second career at Nucor, Tony kept telling me about the company, the compensation, and the culture. He would often call me up and encourage me to apply for a job there. Honestly, I blew him off as this would require a move, and I wasn't ready for that. However, the time finally did come for me to make a change. So, I ultimately listened to my best buddy's advice, applied, tested, interviewed, interviewed again, and interviewed once more. Then I began a new career with one of the greatest companies in North America. What I soon learned was that it is not just a workplace.

At the time of this writing, I have been employed at Nucor for over eleven years, and although it is hard work, in often crazy extreme conditions, I have learned that it's not just about the work. It's not just about making steel. It's not just about taking care of our customers. It's not even just about turning a profit. It's about family. It's about watching out for each other every hour of every shift of every day to make sure we do what's right, and we go home to our loved ones the same way we left them. It's about taking the time to know whom you are working with. It's about caring about them as people. It's about being the keeper of your brothers and sisters. It's about family.

It wasn't long before I learned what it was like to be a part of this family. I heard talk of guys getting sick or being in the hospital, and leadership and peers would visit them. They would check on their family. I had heard that they treated you like family here. I learned what that looked like a few years after I started.

I began my career with Nucor at our Memphis mill, where my family education first began taking shape. I met so many great people there. I got the chance to work with a team of people that supported the American Cancer Society and this thing called Relay for Life. Tony was greatly involved in organizing and helping put together an annual event as a Relay fundraiser; I just pitched in and helped as well. The amount of work and energy the team put in while preparing and running a massive fundraiser blew me away. These people cared about what they were doing and for whom they were doing it. I later found out that several teammates we worked with there were cancer survivors themselves. It was personal for them. Because it was personal for them, it was personal for us also. Every year we put hours of effort in and raise thousands and thousands of dollars to support ACS and its fight against cancer. This year, even though I am no longer with our Memphis division, I will be going back there to that same fundraiser that Tony is still running point on and show my support as a team member from our Louisiana Division and will be bringing a team of folks up there with me. It's what we do. We take care of each other and look out for the other guys. The event this year, as every year prior, includes a golf tournament named for a man who lost his life on the job just before I started with the company.

There's a kicker this year. A new name has been added to the Memorial Golf Tournament. One of the guys who devoted countless hours to put on the Memphis event was a cancer survivor himself and passed away this past year. Jamie and his wife, Susie, worked tirelessly with their real family and work-family year in and year out to ensure the success of this event. This year's tournament is also named for Jamie and promises to be the grandest event yet.

Now that I am a team member at our Louisiana plant, I have gained an even greater understanding of what our culture at Nucor means. I am one of those teammates that landed in the hospital emergency room one night. Yes, I received a visit and several calls from my then-operations manager and numerous other teammates. We have had numerous examples of what it means to be part of something bigger than you here in Louisiana. We have had teammates lose family members, husbands, wives, and even children, and the NSLA family was right there in the trenches with them. We have had teammates with children and grandchildren diagnosed with cancer; the NSLA family was there with them. We have had teammates lose their homes during hurricanes and floods, and our NSLA family was right there with them, walking the journey alongside and holding them up when they needed that support.

My teammate, Anitra, whose daughter Bailee was diagnosed with DIPG, a super-aggressive brain cancer, also learned this firsthand. Her Nucor family rallied around Bailee and became Bailee's Brigade supporting her in her battle and fighting for her when she didn't have the strength. She could lean on her family and her Nucor family and did just that through her walk every step until her last days and beyond. Bailee's Brigade is still here!

My grandson, Colton, whom I introduced to you in my first book, was walked alongside during his journey through a brain tumor and cancer treatment at twenty months old. Upon learning of his diagnosis, the family here in Louisiana stepped up with fundraisers of raffles, food sales, and the sort and supported our daughter and her family through the journey. They became Colton's Crusaders and rallied around him in support and love. Colton's Crusaders are still here!

The examples just shared are only a fraction of the countless times this Nucor family has stood in the gap for our teammates and family. It truly is second nature when one of our team is going through something are not going through it alone. It's just what we do and who we are. One of the greatest blessings one can ever receive is the love and support of those around him. We have that here. People care about each other, not just in words but in deeds as well. I'm sure you have heard the saying that actions speak louder than words. At NUCOR, those actions are as loud as 102,000 screaming and cheering LSU Fans on a Saturday night!

If you are ever blessed to be among people like this, I pray you cherish the moments and embrace the opportunity to work alongside that family. Every workplace is not special like this. Every workplace is not filled with caring, selfless people. Every workplace does not have a mindset of always growing, expanding, and living our culture. I am grateful for the ability to be a part of such a winning team and even more grateful to my best buddy, Tony, for never giving up on telling me about this place he had found. A place where even an everyday Joe can be somebody special and be treated as such. I hope you have found or one day you do find such a place. A place filled with people that always have your back, just as family does. It's not just a workplace. It's a family!

Suicide – The Aftermath

Do not be overly wicked, Nor be foolish: Why should you die before your time?

Ecclesiastes 7:17

The untimely loss of life is, in a word, sorrowful. Expediting one's untimely death by taking one's own life has far-reaching effects that leave deep wounds in one's soul. As I mentioned in another short story, my father did just that. My daddy decided, for whatever reason, that he could not face life as it was any longer, and there was no possible way to go on. In this single act of selfishness, he set in motion emotions we, as a family, never even realized we had.

I remember answering the door that Saturday morning at around 7:00 a.m. I was eighteen years old and nine days shy of graduating high school. The excitement and anticipation of graduation day were at the forefront of my mind, and it would be a fantastic time in my life. This was all about to change. We were all still asleep, and when I heard the knock, I got up to answer it. There, standing outside the door to our kitchen, stood two gentlemen. They were both dressed in suits, and one held a sheet of paper, a photocopy of my daddy's driver's license. Mom and Dad were separated, and Dad was living in an apartment, unbeknownst to me, with his girlfriend. I had a sinking feeling that this was not a good visit. The men told me they were detectives with the police department and asked if my mom was home. By this time, she had made her way from her bedroom, slipped on her robe, and let the detectives inside. We walked through the kitchen into the living room, and as I remember, they calmly and emotionlessly told my mom and me that my dad was deceased. My mom crumbled immediately, crying a haunting cry, the kind of cry that comes deep from one's soul. I rushed to hold her, and as she was sobbing, my younger sisters and brother came into the living room. The detectives then let us know what they knew. My father had shot himself in the head with a 22-caliber handgun while lying in his bed in the apartment where he was staying. I was in immediate disbelief, and here's why.

Earlier that week, I saw my dad in town while driving, and we both pulled into a nearby parking lot. I got out of my car and sat in his work truck with him, and we talked for thirty minutes or so. He told me how things were getting better for him at work. He had just started a new job a couple of weeks prior and had already been promoted. He seemed genuinely excited, and even though he and his mom were living apart, he was hopeful. He seemed hopeful that things were turning around. We continued talking and just kind of hanging out, and as we left each other, we told each other, "I love you." This was the last time I would ever see him alive.

The news of my dad's suicide was devastating to our family. I am the oldest son of four children. I have a sister two years younger than me and a brother and sister five years younger. When dad decided to put that gun to his head, he left an eighteen-year-old son, a sixteen-year-old daughter, and thirteen-year-old twins without a father. He permanently left the four children I know he loved and a wife who truly loved him. This decision would ultimately cause hardships and life lessons we were all not ready to face.

I remember my dad was almost always at my baseball games. We played our summer ball season at Alex Box Stadium in Baton Rouge. As I would be warming up on the field, I would look into the stands, and he would usually be there unless he couldn't get away from work. He would always be in the same spot, leaning against a handrail, holding a red Coca-Cola paper cup, as he watched me play a game I so enjoyed. After his death, I still had a season of summer baseball to play before leaving to serve in the Army. I had already enlisted two months before his death and was waiting to ship out for basic training.

Try as I might, I searched for normalcy that was not available. I remember every summer game, as I was warming up on the field before the game, looking into the stands, and seeing my dad standing there in the same spot he always stood. He was wearing the same clothes: a green pair of slacks, a white shirt with green and yellow piping, and leaning on the same handrail holding the same red Coca-Cola cup every game. This freaked me out. I would stop throwing for a minute, shake my head to clear the cobwebs, look back, and he was gone. I told very few people about this and told nobody about it until a few years later. I just dealt with it.

I wonder what things my siblings had to deal with. I wonder what their minds allowed them to see that wasn't there. In three months, they lost their dad, and their big brother was also gone away. We are not a family that talks about things like this, and now I know that's not good. I cannot imagine what growing up, in their most formidable years, as teenage survivors of a family member that took his own life was like for them. These thoughts are still very clear in my mind, yet I choose not to talk about them. I guess one could say I am still bitter about it.

I'm especially bitter about the hardship this put on my mom, who has since passed away from pancreatic cancer. She never remarried, and she was the rock that held her children together through all the hardships she walked through because of this terrible event. Mom had never worked out of the home. She watched a few children from time to time but never held a job until she was alone with three children to raise. She never even had a driver's license. From what I understand, my dad had told her there was no need for one. So, after her husband's death, she got a job, walked about 3/4 of a mile to it every day, and walked home. After I shipped off to basic training, I set up an allotment that was sent to her every month to help her with some money to provide for my brother and sisters. She didn't ask me to; I just did it. Mom was a survivor. She persevered. She was a loving mother to her children who did everything she could to provide for her children. She was not a quitter. She was soft and tender but had a lioness's strong will and determination. I believe we all have ended up okay because of her selflessness, determination, and unconditional love for her children. That's not to say we haven't had our battles and our demons to fight off, but we are better adults today because of the strength and power she mustered during this tough time.

I know there are things she had to deal with that I will never know. I know she was dealt a crappy hand that day in May of 1982. I know she never expected to be a widow due to suicide. I know there are things my siblings dealt with that I may never know of either. I know they didn't expect their dad to take his own life and neither did I. But somehow, we managed to deal with it and press on even though there were times we just wanted to give up. The sting of suicide does not go away completely. The unanswered questions remain—the *What if* thoughts still randomly show up. I remember times when I would break down in tears years later, and once my tears stopped, I would wonder what life would be like if he was still here. When my children were born, I wondered if dad would have been happy. When they were playing baseball as children, just as I did, I would wonder if dad would be there watching them as he watched me, leaning on the handrail and holding that red Coca-Cola cup.

So many questions go unanswered when we lose someone. But it seems that so many more go unanswered when we lose someone to suicide.

Please remember your loved ones should you ever be at what you think is the end of your road. Please reach out for help. Please let someone know what's going on. People care. You are worthy, and you matter. There are people in your life that you matter to. There are people in your life that love you. No matter what you go through, you can come to the other side victorious. God has a plan for your life, and I assure you that plan does not include you stepping in and overriding His plan. You were created for greatness and have an impact zone to impact positively. I'm just being real right now. Here me when I tell you. If you have thought of taking things into your own hands, DON'T! The aftermath you would leave in your wake will haunt those that love you forever. So, reach out and be there for your loved ones. Reach out, grab whatever piece of lifeline you can grab, and be that overcomer! I believe in you! You can and you will!

You Can Do It! Don't Quit!

Now no chastening seems to be joyful for the present, but painful; nevertheless, afterward it yields the peaceable fruit of righteousness to those who have been trained by it. Hebrews 12:11

The year 1982 brought forth much change in my life. It brought joy, happiness, pain, uncertainty, final chapters, and new beginnings. As I reflect on this year, I'm reminded of all of this and more. In 1982, I graduated high school, lost my father to a self-inflicted gunshot wound, played my last season of baseball with all of my friends, and turned eighteen. I was legal age to drink alcohol, which caused many poor decisions. I enlisted in the Army, graduated boot camp, and began what would be a twenty-four-year career in the military. It was one of those defining years in my life that issued challenges, struggles, growth, and victory.

I was due to graduate high school on May 24, and it was anticipated to be a happy time. The complete happiness was not to be. It was on May 15, just nine days before graduation, that my father took his own life, the story of which you just read. The normal joy and happiness were just not there. I was due to ship out to boot camp for the Army on July 28 and with my dad's death still fresh I took a short-term job as a laborer in a local oil refinery and worked there until I shipped out for boot.

When I arrived at Ft Jackson, South Carolina, I had no idea what to expect, but I quickly realized this was not summer camp nor a vacation. This was a real deal with instantaneous screwing of our minds, physical pain, and a complete breaking down of my mind and body so that I could be rebuilt and retrained the Army way. I arrived by bus in the middle of the night to what was to be my new home for the next eight weeks or however long I would be around. I was abruptly met by a crew of screaming, yelling Neanderthals that barked out order after order, command after command, which nobody was arriving that night could have anticipated. All I could think about was not to make eye contact, try to blend in, and for goodness' sake, not draw any attention to myself. That philosophy was short-lived as the crazy crew of brown hat-wearing terrorists generously gave their attention to each maggot that dared to enter the gates of hell of a basic training post. For what seemed like hours, we were belittled, shamed, screamed at, and berated with words and vocabulary you don't hear on Sunday mornings at church. We were finally introduced to our barracks, a forty-eight-man open bay bunkhouse where we would stay until our real drill sergeants would pick us up and escort us to our more permanent home away from home, as this was only the reception battalion. Reception battalion? It was not a very pleasant reception, and it became clear to me rather quickly that I had a lot to learn about the military.

After about five days, we received our uniforms, fresh haircuts, massive amounts of immunizations, and more verbal abuse; we were introduced to our drill sergeant. This guy stood about 5'7", wore mirrored wire frame sunglasses, and was built in a perfect V-shape from his feet through his broad shoulders. Staff Sergeant Jackson was as rough and tough as they come and immediately, for some reason, singled me out. He got in my face, the brim of his brown round (drill sergeant hat) tapping me on my forehead as he whispered in a calm, matter-of-fact voice, "You're not going to make it, fat boy." I honestly didn't know how to take that. Why did he single me out? Did he know me already? Did he know I was already doubting myself and questioning my decision to enlist? It was at that point that something clicked in my brain. At that point, I made the mental decision that he would not break me. I was not going to quit. The competitor in me would not allow this guy to run me off. I soon discovered those brief thoughts would come and go as I went through the process of becoming Army green.

Early morning wake-ups to noisy trash can rattling, whistles, and relentless hollering were my norm for the next eight weeks. Our slumber was often interrupted by an impromptu physical training session, commonly called PT, which would include flutter kicks, push-ups, jumping jacks, duck walks, sit-ups, and other forms of torture they could dream up. As the weeks rolled on, my physical demands increased, even though my strength also increased. When I first got to the beautiful Ft. Jackson training facility, I could barely do twenty push-ups. Now I could do upwards of fifty to sixty in one stretch.

We had training classes where we received instruction on how to apply basic first aid, basic map reading and land navigation, weapons training, as well as the good ole UCMJ, the Uniformed Code of Military Justice, which is a whole new set of laws that we as soldiers must abide by. While in the classroom phases, we were even afforded breaks! Yes, we were given a break of ten minutes for every fifty minutes of classroom instruction. These breaks were loaded with fun. We could go outside, get into formation, don our rucksacks, and get down in the front leaning rest position, which is the start position for push-ups for the entire time of our breaks. Oh, and we were fortunate enough to be allowed to do this "rest" in a gravel parking lot. What fun, right? But still, I kept in mind my first encounter with SSG Jackson and vowed to myself that I would not quit. I would not allow this guy to break me.

As our training continued, quite a few guys in my platoon gave up and opted out. They let the instructors in their heads and just couldn't cope. One of these times was when we were awakened at 2:00 a.m. to the sound of a bullhorn screaming over it. We immediately dressed into our battle dress uniforms, laced up our boots, grabbed our headgear, and went downstairs, where we noticed the entire company, all four platoons, had all done the same thing. We were then issued weapons that we had not yet qualified with. We were told that attacks were going on in Beirut, Lebanon, and we were being deployed that day. I was like, this is crazy! What the heck? Are you kidding me? Guys were shaking, some were crying, some had a blank stare, and some showed no emotion. As for me, I was wondering if this was happening. After about three hours of this preparation and mind games, we were told that it had been called off and our normal training schedule would be picked up. These are the types of mind games played in all military schools I had ever been to in all my twenty-four years of service—just plain craziness to the normal civilian mind but essential character-building to those of a military mindset. I still maintained my resolve, obviously, and refused to quit.

Another trying time was our fourteen-mile forced road march, complete with full battle gear, weapons, and sixty-pound rucksacks on our backs. This was the most physically demanding day I had in basic. I quickly developed blisters on the heels of both of my feet and was in pain the entire time. We were to remain silent the entire time we were on this march. The only voices I heard were inside my head. These voices told me to quit, give up, and go home. However, they were met with other voices inside me that told me to keep going. They asked me what I would tell my family, friends, and all of those who had wished me well as they hugged me goodbye. These voices asked me how I would keep my head held high. They asked me how I could quit when so many others before me did not. They asked if I thought those who went before me into combat were any different than I was. They told me loudly don't quit, don't give up; you can do it! For the remainder of the road march, I battled within myself whether to hang it up or to push through and before I could settle my mind's argument, we were approaching our barracks again, and the march from hell was complete. I had done it! I had pushed through! I did not quit! There was no stopping me now.

As the last couple of weeks quickly passed, my mindset changed; I was designated squad leader and eventually received recognition as an honor graduate for our basic training class. I had not only pushed through, but I excelled. This is truly something I could be proud of. This was just the beginning of a long, challenging, yet rewarding career serving our great country. I grew so much in 1982. It was a year that truly formed me. It is said that we grow in adversity and challenges and when we are out of our comfort zone. That year was truly uncomfortable, and yes, growth is what happened. I am grateful for that growth, and I am grateful for the challenge, as the happenings in 1982 helped shape me into the man I remain today.

An Investment with Great Returns

Wherever your treasure is, there your heart will be also. Matthew 6:21

Have you ever looked at your retirement portfolio, 401(k), Roth IRA, or stocks and just watched the decline? I'm not a financial expert, but I can tell you from experience that when world markets are declining, my zest for investing does as well. I don't want to invest in something that is currently losing. I just don't. We begin to look to the experts for advice. We begin to give greater value to what their opinions are. We begin to believe what they tell us. When our marriage starts to decline, do we respond the same way?

I want to add encouragement and practical steps to improve your marriage portfolio. I will share with you three practical steps that my wife Michelle and I have taken and found to be very productive and provide those great returns we look for in an investment. The concept is a simple one. Here are three things: prayer, forgiveness, and time.

Michelle and I have found that a consistent prayer life has been crucial to our growth as a couple. Do we pray together every day? Honestly, we do not. Truthfully, we make a conscious choice to pray or not. We give priority in our lives to the things we deem important. So, on those days that we do not take time out to pray together, what we are saying is that this time we wanted to set aside to put our marriage on the altar and pray jointly for our marriage, our day, our family, as well as strength, forgiveness, and protection is not important enough to us. We choose to go it alone. Friends, that choice can be harmful to our marriage portfolio. The strength we receive when we daily commit our marriage to God and seek his protection is equal to that of superhuman strength. When we consciously decide to put aside everything else for just a moment and pray, we invest in something that will ultimately pay huge dividends in our marriage.

We are laying the groundwork for our day together and coming together as one to our Lord. This may not come naturally or easily. There will be times when Satan steps in and wants us to put priorities on other things. As I write this, let me pause for a moment and do just that. Michelle and I have let our day start without praying together. We are about to invest these next few minutes together and pray for our day as one, and I encourage you to do the same.

Okay, I am back and equipped to move forward. Prayer time is our time to spend together in God's presence jointly. It is a time when we speak gratitude and thanks as well as lift needs and requests. The key is to do this together. One person may do all the praying, or both may alternate prayers. In our case, Michelle is uncomfortable with spoken prayer, even in my presence. That's not to say she doesn't pray because she does pray silently as she thinks her prayers. We understand that I do not ask her to pray aloud. I've been there, done that, and yes, lived with the fallout of such a poor decision. Men, respect your wife's comfort level and although we might encourage, never push. She's not a young bird that needs to be pushed out of her nest to fly; she can fly on her own and will. Our job as husbands is to love, cherish, and support her. Prayer is the number one priority when we are investing in our marriage. Without that consistent prayer life, we are simply reducing the return on the investment in our marriage.

Our second priority is forgiveness. When we forgive, God's grace will flow freely upon our marriage. One of the first things that come to our mind about forgiving our spouse is how often we forgive. How often?

Well, I look at it this way. I have been a recipient of many acts of forgiveness. Forgiveness does not mean there are no consequences for your actions. When we seek forgiveness, we must understand that a couple of things must happen. We must truly ask and seek that forgiveness by confessing whatever we have done. This can be very difficult to do.

Here's an example of what that might look like. Let's say I had gone out with the guys from work to grab a bite. What began as a quick eating bite soon became an extended drinking session with the boys. I chose to hang out with them and returned home several hours later without a phone call to my wife. When I get home, I'm confronted by the woman that loves me, and now I must face the music. I decided to do something I knew would not go over well with my wife, but I did it anyway. Now comes the request for forgiveness. I don't think this request will be received immediately and without fallout, for one minute. Remember, I chose to do something that showed disrespect and put my wife and our marriage on a lower priority than what I said. Actions speak louder than words; now, my actions are screaming! We cannot, and should not, expect immediate forgiveness from our spouse. Understand that it is a process. We often make those choices that hurt them, and healing takes time.

Often, that hurt is so deep that it takes a long time to receive that forgiveness. When we wrong our spouse, we must understand that we have done something that can spiral out of control. It will be like a blister on our heel that keeps coming back because we keep wearing the same socks and shoes. We need to make a change. That change is turning away from hanging out with the guys after work. That change might be putting that bottle of booze down. That change might be to be more intentional about how we spend our time. When we turn away from something coming between us and the person we married, we give them the priority they deserve. We are giving them the priority that says to them, I love you, and you mean more to me than any bottle of booze or any group of guys that want me to hang out and rob us of our time together. Forgiveness will come as we place our priorities back in line. So, keep praying and equipping your marriage to fight off those attacks from the predator searching for its easy prey.

Invest time in your marriage. As we said in the beginning, our third priority is time. We see in the preceding paragraph that forgiveness takes time. If we apply the law of compound effect to our marriage, we will eventually see the positive results we are looking for. Our financial investment accounts do not mature immediately, nor do they show an increase exponentially from one day to the next. It takes consistent deposits over an extended period of time.[7] Similarly, our marriage works the same way. The more we make the deposits of love, kind words, encouragement, speak our spouse's love language, spend time together, and many other things, we will see over time, the return on the investment in our marriage becomes huge![8] This is exciting!

When we get to a point in our marriage where we can reflect on where we used to be, look back at what we have gone through (the mistreatment, mean words, acts of defiance, lack of prayer time, times of no forgiveness, times of resentment and selfishness), we can see the negatives disappear and be replaced by their opposites (kind words, acts of agreement, increased prayer time, forgiveness, acceptance, and selflessness).[9] We find that we are now living our lives to serve our spouses. We actively seek ways to make them happy and bring them joy. We get excited about spending time together, connecting on even the simplest of terms. We get excited about weekly or monthly date nights. We get excited about doing something with our spouse that we don't necessarily get into, but we know they do. We put our needs and desires behind those of our husbands or wives and realize they are doing the same thing. Time spent with each other reconnects you and brings you back in line with what is important to both of you.

When we intentionally spend time with each other, we tell each other you are important to me. I value you and cherish our marriage. You make me want to get better. I thank you for making me better, and I am grateful for your love. I'm grateful for your forgiveness. I'm grateful for your support. I'm grateful for your friendship. I'm grateful to you. We spend time on the things that have the greatest priority to us. So, when we carve out time to pour into the investment of our marriage, we cannot help but get great returns! Time is a valuable commodity. We don't know how much time we have. Make the most of your time and invest it wisely. Invest it in your relationships. Invest it properly and reap the benefits. Suppose you want a great return on your investment; a place that investment vehicle where it can grow the most. Place it in prayer, forgiveness, and time. I encourage you to make your marriage growth a priority by applying these three principles. I challenge you to make your marriage better by investing in it, and I pray for God's blessings on your relationship as you do so.

Turkey Taco Lettuce Wraps

Ingredients

- ➢ 2 tbsp. roasted garlic avocado oil
- ➢ 1 pinch Kosher Salt
- ➢ 3/4 cup red onion, finely chopped
- ➢ 6 garlic cloves, finely chopped
- ➢ 3 tsp. chili powder
- ➢ 2 tsp. smoked paprika
- ➢ 1-1/2 cups whole kernel corn
- ➢ 1 15.5 oz can black beans, drained

- ➤ Romaine lettuce leaves

Toppings Ingredients

- ➤ fresh cilantro, chopped
- ➤ queso fresco cheese, crumbled
- ➤ avocado, diced
- ➤ salsa

Directions

1. Pour two tablespoons roasted garlic avocado oil into a large skillet and heat at med-high heat.
2. Add ground turkey to the skillet and season with a pinch of salt.
3. Brown the turkey meat while breaking it up into small, crumbled pieces.
4. Remove browned turkey from the skillet, place it on a pan and set aside.
5. Add a touch more olive oil to the skillet, then add the chopped onion and garlic. Lower the heat to med-low and sauté. Stir often to ensure it does not scorch. Sauté until onions are transparent.
6. Add turkey back to the skillet along with the chili powder and smoked paprika, return heat to medium-high and cook for about five minutes. Add a little water to the turkey if needed, as it is lean poultry and could dry out quickly.
7. Add the corn and black beans, reduce heat, mix well, and occasionally stir as you cook for another four to five minutes.
8. Place Romaine lettuce leaves on a plate and spoon the taco meat

and beans onto the lettuce.

9. Top with any or all of your favorite toppings and serve.

Street Corn Dip

Ingredients

- ➢ 1 tbsp. caramelized onion avocado oil
- ➢ 1 tbsp. roasted garlic olive oil
- ➢ 3 cups whole-kernel corn
- ➢ 6 cloves fresh garlic, pressed
- ➢ 2 small jalapenos, seeded and finely chopped (optional)
- ➢ 1/2 cup red Mexican onion, chopped
- ➢ 1/2 cup queso fresco cheese, crumbled
- ➢ 1/4 cup fresh cilantro, chopped
- ➢ 1 tsp. smoked paprika

- ➢ 1/2 cup sour cream
- ➢ 1-1/2 tsp. chili powder
- ➢ Juice from 1/2 lime
- ➢ Juice from 1/2 lemon

Directions

1. Pour avocado oil and roasted garlic olive oil into a skillet and preheat on med-high heat.
2. When the skillet is hot, add corn it and sauté for fifteen minutes or so, stirring often to avoid sticking. You are sautéing the corn to create a light char on the kernels, so adjust your fire accordingly. You don't want to burn but want a light browning on the kernels.
3. Once you achieve desired char, reduce the fire, and add your pressed garlic, stir and cook for a couple of minutes.
4. In a separate bowl, add all your other ingredients.
5. Add corn and garlic mixture to the bowl.
6. Blend well and serve.

Note: This dip is a very versatile dish and can be served as a nice side dish, hot or cold, and can also be used as a tortilla chip dip.

Meat & Cheese Rollups

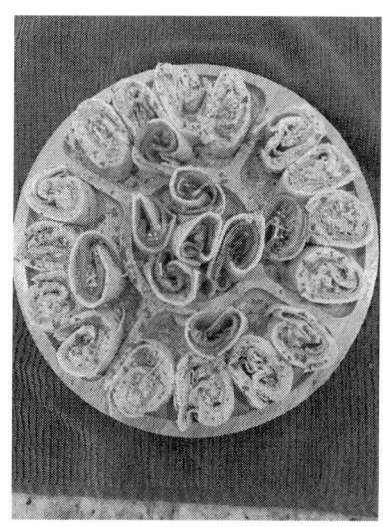

Ingredients

- 8 oz. block of cream cheese
- 1/2 lb. of sandwich meat, thinly sliced (ham, turkey, roast beef)
- 6-10 medium-sized soft tortilla shells
- 1 heaping tsp. of smoked paprika
- 1 tsp. smokey garlic and onion seasoning
- 1/4 cup fresh chives, finely chopped
- 1/4 cup Parmesan cheese, grated
- Pinch of Cajun seasoning
- 1/4 cup parsley, chopped

Directions

1. Allow cream cheese to soften, then place in a mixing bowl.
2. Add seasonings (smoked paprika, garlic and onion seasoning, and chives) to cream cheese and mix well.
3. Lightly spread a layer of cream cheese onto a soft tortilla shell.
4. Place a layer of sandwich meat on the bed of cream cheese.
5. Add a couple of pinches of grated Parmesan cheese.
6. Roll up the tortilla shell, adding a bit of cream cheese at the flap to help secure the roll.
7. Place in a plastic storage bag.
8. Repeat this process until all of the cream cheese mixture is used.
9. Seal the bag tightly and place it in the refrigerator for one to two hours until ready to serve.
10. Remove from the refrigerator, place roll-ups on the cutting surface, and slice into one to one-and-a-half-inch slices.
11. Place roll-up slices on a serving tray or charcuterie board.
12. Lightly sprinkle a touch of Cajun seasoning over the top of the rollups.
13. Garnish with loosely chopped parsley and serve.

Buttermilk Blue Cheese Dressing

Ingredients

- ➢ 3/4 cup buttermilk
- ➢ 1-1/2 cups blue cheese, crumbled
- ➢ 2 tbsp. mayonnaise
- ➢ 1 tbsp. olive oil
- ➢ Dash of hot sauce
- ➢ 2 tbsp. lemon juice
- ➢ Dash Worcestershire sauce
- ➢ 1 tsp. white pepper
- ➢ 1/4 tsp. dill weed

- 1/4 cup chives
- 5 cloves of garlic, pressed
- 1 tsp. garlic juice

Directions

1. In a medium size mixing bowl, combine buttermilk, blue cheese, mayonnaise, olive oil, hot sauce, lemon juice, and Worcestershire sauce.
2. Gently stir to mix thoroughly, being careful not to crumble the chunks of blue cheese too much.
3. Add the dry seasonings: white pepper, dill, chives, and garlic. Gently stir well, taste, and add additional seasonings to your liking.

Note: You can add a little buttermilk and mayonnaise to loosen the dressing up. Add a little cornstarch and additional blue cheese to thicken according to your preference.

4. I recommend keeping this salad dressing in the refrigerator until ready to use. However, I would not keep past five to seven days. Once it gets there, just toss it out and make a fresh batch.
5. Cover the container tightly and place it in the refrigerator.

Buttermilk Ranch Dressing

Ingredients

- ➢ 1/2 cup mayonnaise
- ➢ 1/3 cup sour cream
- ➢ 1/2 cup buttermilk
- ➢ 1 tbsp. lemon juice
- ➢ 1 tsp. Worcestershire sauce
- ➢ 1 tbsp. dill weed
- ➢ 1 tbsp. parsley
- ➢ 1 tbsp. chives

- 1 tsp. onion powder
- 1 tsp. garlic pepper seasoning
- 1 tsp. Cajun/Creole seasoning

Directions

1. Mix the mayonnaise, sour cream, buttermilk, lemon juice, and Worcestershire sauce in a medium-sized mixing bowl. Use a wire whisk to stir and mix well. You will notice as you begin stirring that it is a little clumpy. Keep the faith, and stir until you achieve a smooth and creamy consistency.
2. Add your dry seasonings and mix well. Dill weed, parsley, chives, onion powder, garlic pepper seasoning, and Cajun/Creole seasoning and stir until mixed.
3. Season to taste, and chill in the refrigerator covered and sealed.

Note:

Fresh homemade salad dressings should only be kept in the refrigerator for up to three to four days, so make sure you make only about the quantity you will need. This is a very simple and quick recipe, so it's no issue to make it fresh every time!

Shepherd's Pie

Ingredients

- 5 lbs. potatoes, peeled and cubed
- 2 tbsp. unsalted butter
- 1-1/2 lbs. ground chuck
- beef seasoning
- 1 pinch of Kosher salt
- 2 pinches of course ground black pepper
- 2 tbsp. avocado oil, caramelized onion flavor
- 1 large onion, finely chopped
- 1 cup carrots, chopped
- 1 15 oz. can whole kernel sweet corn
- 1 15 oz. can sweet peas

- 1 10.5 oz. can cream of mushroom soup
- 1/2 cup beef broth
- 2 tbsp. all-purpose flour
- 1 cup shredded cheddar cheese

Directions

1. Place cubed potatoes in a large pot with the water level about one inch above the potatoes. Add two tablespoons of unsalted butter and just a dash of salt. Bring to a boil, lower heat, and let simmer for about fifteen minutes, or until potatoes are tender but still a bit firm.
2. Strain the potatoes and pour them into a mixing bowl where you can now mash them, salt and pepper to taste, and set aside.
3. Place chopped carrots in a small pot with water, one tablespoon of unsalted butter, and a dash of salt. Bring to a boil, lower the heat and let simmer for about ten minutes. You want them to be firm, not mushy.
4. Strain the carrots and set them aside.
5. In a large skillet (I generally use cast iron.), pour one tablespoon of caramelized onion-flavored avocado oil. Once heated, add one and a half pounds of ground chuck. At this point, you can add your favorite beef seasoning to the meat. Stir until browned; remove from skillet. Place on a paper towel-lined pan, and cover with additional paper towels to soak up excess grease.
6. Using the same skillet we browned the meat in, and add another tablespoon of caramelized onion-flavored avocado oil. Once

heated, add onions, carrots, peas, and corn. Sauté until onions become transparent.

7. Add cream of mushroom soup and stir to mix the soup throughout the veggies medley.
8. Pour a half cup of beef broth into a cup and gently stir two tablespoons of all-purpose flour into the broth until it is all dissolved.
9. Pour the broth/flour mixture into the veggies and stir. This will allow the mixture to thicken a bit as it cooks.
10. Preheat oven to 375 degrees.
11. Once the veggie medley is cooked, pour over the layer of ground chuck we placed in that 9 x 13 baking dish.
12. Add a layer of mashed potatoes.
13. Place a 9 x 13 baking dish into the preheated oven.

Tip: You might want to place your 9 x 13 dish on a baking sheet to catch any overflow created while baking. This will help keep your oven a bit cleaner.

14. Bake at 375 degrees for thirty minutes.
15. Remove from the oven and sprinkle shredded cheese evenly over the potatoes. Place back in the oven for five minutes.
16. Remove from the oven and let sit for about ten minutes before serving.

Spaghetti for 50

Ingredients

- 8 lbs. ground chuck
- 4 lbs. ground mild Italian sausage
- 1 tbsp. caramelized onion olive oil
- 1 tbsp. smoky garlic avocado oil
- 48 oz. Cajun trinity
- 4 tbsp. minced garlic
- 9 15 oz. cans tomato sauce
- 9 14.5 oz. can diced tomatoes
- 6 (6 oz.) cans tomato paste

- ➤ 3 (32 oz.) cartons of beef broth
- ➤ 1/2 cup dry Italian seasoning
- ➤ 1/4 cup dry smoked roasted garlic and onion seasoning
- ➤ 2 tbsp. granulated sugar
- ➤ 1 cup grated Parmesan cheese

Directions

1. Heat a cast-iron pot (For this recipe and other large quantity recipes, I use a ten-gallon cast-iron pot and propane burner.) and put ground chuck and Italian ground sausage in the pot to brown.
2. Strain grease from meat and remove from pot. Place in a heavily lined bowl to help soak up the excess grease that has not strained out.
3. Remove excess grease from the pot.
4. Pour avocado oil and olive oil into the pot.
5. Add trinity and cook down until onions are wilted and soft, almost transparent.
6. Add minced garlic.
7. Stir vegetables well.
8. Add meat back to the pot and mix well with vegetables.
9. Add six cans of tomato sauce, six cans of diced tomatoes, three cans of tomato paste, Italian seasoning, dry smoked roasted garlic and onion seasoning, and two boxes of beef broth.
10. Stir sauce well.
11. Allow cooking on low to medium heat for about twenty minutes.
12. Taste for seasoning and add more to taste.

13. Add the remaining three cans of tomato sauce, diced tomatoes, tomato paste, and beef broth.
14. Stir well, lower heat to the lowest possible setting, and allow to cook for a couple of hours, stirring occasionally.
15. Finally, about fifteen minutes before serving, add sugar and grated Parmesan and stir well.

Red Beans & Rice – The Monday Special

Ingredients

- ➢ 2 lbs. red kidney beans
- ➢ 1-2 lbs. smoked pork (hocks, butts, or ham)
- ➢ 2 tbsp. of caramelized onion avocado oil
- ➢ 1 large Vidalia onion
- ➢ 2 cloves garlic
- ➢ 1-2 tsp. Cajun seasoning
- ➢ 4 cups rice
- ➢ 8 cups water
- ➢ Kosher salt

Directions

1. Pour dry beans into a bowl, cover with water, lid the bowl, and place in the refrigerator overnight.

Note: beans will absorb water as they soak, so you will need to add water once or twice as they soak.

2. Some beans will float as they soak; go ahead and remove the floaters and discard them.
3. After the beans have soaked, use a colander and drain the water from the beans. Rinse them thoroughly and leave them in a colander while preparing the seasonings.
4. Place a large pot on the stove over med-med/high heat and pour your caramelized onion avocado oil into the pot.
5. Chop your onion to your liking. For beans, I generally go with a loose chop (one that is not as fine as I would use in my gumbo).
6. Mince your garlic cloves.
7. Add garlic, onion, and a little Cajun seasoning to the pot and sauté until the onions are transparent.
8. Add a little water to the pot and stir to mix the seasoning well.
9. Place your smoked pork in the pot, then add your beans.
10. Pour fresh water into the pot until the beans are covered with water.
11. Turn the stove burner on medium, bring to a boil, cover the pot, reduce heat to medium-low, and check on them in an hour.
12. You might need to add more water and occasionally stir as you cook the beans.

13. I cook my beans on low heat all day for about six hours.
14. Once the meat cooks off the bones, I will remove the bone from the beans and anything that is not meat or bean. (Sometimes you will have hocks with skin or fatty tissue.)
15. After about four hours, I take about a cup of beans, mash them well with a fork, and pour them back into the pot. This serves as a natural thickener and thickens up our beans nicely.
16. This is when I cook my rice: Use two cups of rice to four cups of water. I always use a two-to-one ratio of water to rice, adding a little salt to the water and just a small dab of butter.
17. Bring water to a boil, add rice and stir well.
18. Return rice to a boil, cover the pot and lower the heat to simmer.
19. Let all the water cook out of the rice. It's ok to stir the rice occasionally as it simmers and you cook out the water. Just realize that every time you open the lid, you are letting the steam escape and affecting the time and temp of the cook.
20. Once the rice is cooked, strain it and rinse it. This rinses a lot of the excess starch from the rice.
21. Place a little rice in the center of a bowl, ladle some beans and juice over the rice, and serve with some nice French bread so you can sop up all the juice at the end!

Notes

1. Pam Tebow, Ripple Effects: Discover the Miraculous Motivating Power of a Woman's Influence (Carol Stream, Illinois: Tyndale Momentum, 2019).

2. "Abigail (Name)," Wikipedia (Wikimedia Foundation, October 20, 2022), https://en.wikipedia.org/wiki/Abigail_(name)#:

3. "Juvenile Dermatomyositis," Stanford Medicine Children's Health - Lucile Packard Children's Hospital Stanford, accessed November 14, 2022, https://www.stanfordchildrens.org/en/topic/default?id=juvenile-dermatomyositis-90-P01714.

4. *Home Alone*, directed by Christopher Columbus (Twentieth Century Fox, 1990).

5. Art Williams, "'Just Do It,'" James Clear, August 3, 2021, https://jamesclear.com/great-speeches/just-do-it-by-art-williams.

6. "Tradition Definition & Meaning," Merriam-Webster (Merriam-Webster), accessed November 14, 2022, https://www.merriam-webster.com/dictionary/tradition.

7. Brian Tracy, "The 100 Absolutely Unbreakable: Laws of Business Success," O'Reilly Online Learning (Berrett-Koehler Publishers), accessed November 14, 2022, https://www.oreilly.com/library/view/the-100-absolutely/9781576751077/.

8. Dr. Jonathan Ramachenderan, "The Healthy GP," The Healthy GP (blog), January 18, 2016, https://thehealthygp.com/2016/01/18/how-to-use-the-power-of-compounding-to-improve-your-marriage-in-the-early-years/.

9. Dr. Jonathan Ramachenderan, "The Healthy GP," The Healthy GP (blog).

Bibliography

Tebow, Pam. Ripple Effects: Discover the Miraculous Motivating Power of a Woman's Influence. Carol Stream, Illinois: Tyndale Momentum, 2022.

"Abigail (Name)." Wikipedia. Wikimedia Foundation, October 20, 2022. https://en.wikipedia.org/wiki/Abigail_(name)#:

"Juvenile Dermatomyositis." Stanford Medicine Children's Health - Lucile Packard Children's Hospital Stanford. Accessed November 14, 2022. https://www.stanfordchildrens.org/en/topic/default?id=juvenile-dermatomyositis-90-P01714.

Columbus, Chris. 1990. Home Alone. United States: Twentieth Century Fox. DVD.

Williams, Art. "'Just Do It.'" James Clear, August 3, 2021. https://jamesclear.com/great-speeches/just-do-it-by-art-williams.

Merriam-Webster.com Dictionary, s.v. "tradition," accessed November 14, 2022, https://www.merriam-webster.com/dictionary/tradition.

Tracy, Brian. "The 100 Absolutely Unbreakable: Laws of Business Success." O'Reilly Online Learning. Berrett-Koehler Publishers. Accessed November 14, 2022. https://www.oreilly.com/library/view/the-100-absolutely/9781576751077/.

Ramachenderan, Dr. Jonathan. "How to Use the Power of Compounding to Improve Your Marriage in the Early Years." Web log.

The Healthy GP (blog), January 18, 2016. https://thehealthygp.com/2016/01/18/how-to-use-the-power-of-compounding-to-improve-your-marriage-in-the-early-years/.

Made in the USA
Columbia, SC
24 November 2022